EXPONENTIALLY ELEVATE YOUR
LEADERSHIP
IMPACT

A YEARLONG JOURNEY TO REFLECT, STRENGTHEN, AND ELEVATE YOUR LEADERSHIP

(AN INTERACTIVE JOURNAL EXPERIENCE)

DR. STEPHANIE DUGUID

Table of Contents

Introduction

Is This a Book That I Should Pick Up and Read?

Many women in education, often without realizing it, struggle with confidence. They may question their decisions, hesitate to speak up in meetings, or feel unsure about their leadership abilities. Perhaps they collaborate with a supervisor who prioritizes policies and bottom-line results while neglecting the human aspect of leadership. If any of these scenarios sound familiar, then this book is for you. This guide will take you step by step through the process of building confidence, strengthening your voice, and owning your leadership journey. We'll begin with a few foundational activities to help you prepare for the next steps toward authentic and empowered leadership.

Maybe you were once confident in your role, but negative feedback or an unsupportive supervisor made you question your abilities. Let me assure you—we've all been there. I've worked with supervisors who were in leadership positions not because they earned them, but due to favors, politics, or simply being "next in line." Some of them stepped on others to get ahead, never considering the consequences. Others were placed in roles they were completely unprepared for, leaving their teams to train them while navigating the challenges of poor leadership. If you've ever had to manage up, train a supervisor, or work under ineffective leadership, then you understand the struggle. But here's the key: if you remain a positively authentic leader, committed to connecting with and supporting those around you, you will succeed, no matter the challenges.

Overcoming Imposter Syndrome & Stepping Into Your Confidence

One of the biggest challenges for women in leadership is Imposter Syndrome—the feeling that you don't deserve your success, aren't qualified enough, or will be exposed as a fraud. But let me tell you something: Everyone struggles with Imposter Syndrome—from top executives to award-winning actors, from authors to educators, and everyone in between. The truth is, no one ever feels completely "ready" for the next big opportunity. But growth happens when we step outside of our comfort zones, embrace new challenges, and trust in our ability to learn and adapt.

If you're waiting until you feel 100% prepared before taking on a new role, leadership opportunity, or challenge—you'll be waiting forever. The first step is a positive mindset, followed by bold action. This book will help you develop the confidence to make decisions you believe in, stay true to your ethical standards, and lead in a way that prioritizes people over policies. If any of this resonates with you, then this book was written for you.

Who Is This Book For?

This book is for leaders seeking authenticity, impact, and sustainable success through intentional leadership development. Leadership is not about titles, it is about action, influence, and integrity. Some of the most incredible leaders I have encountered hold no formal title at all—yet they lead through collaboration, service, ethical decision-making, and the way they elevate others. True leadership is not confined to a position or an organization; it is how you show up, how you connect, and how you inspire those around you.

If you are wondering, *Is this book for me?* The answer is yes. If you are a seasoned leader still questioning your direction, this book is for you. If you are a new leader, navigating the challenges of stepping into leadership, this book is for you. If you aspire to lead but haven't stepped into a leadership role yet, this book is for you. Whether or not you hold a title, if your goal is to build stronger relationships, lead with confidence, and grow both personally and professionally, this book will guide you through that journey.

The Role of Reflection in Leadership Growth

Throughout this book, reflection will play a key role in your leadership development. Many believe that reflection is only necessary when mistakes happen or challenges arise—a way to course-correct for the future. But reflection is essential for all growth. It is through intentional self-examination that we uncover strengths, recognize patterns, and identify ways to improve. This book will encourage you to pause, reflect, and refine your leadership approach, ensuring that you continue to learn, develop, and lead with purpose. If you are committed to authentic leadership and making a meaningful impact, this book is for you.

Why I Wrote This Book

As you explore this book, you might wonder, *Where did all this come from, and why is she writing it?* The answer lies in my own leadership journey, a journey deeply influenced by my mother, a lifelong educator and mentor.

I have been in leadership for over 30 years, though I did not initially plan to be in this role. My mother was a teacher, mentor, guide, and advocate for her students, often going far beyond the classroom to support them. She helped students find jobs, filled out their applications, and even took in those who needed a safe place to stay. She met her students where they were, encouraging and supporting them in ways that shaped their futures. Leadership, in its truest form, was something she demonstrated every day—not for recognition, but because it was simply the right thing to do. I saw firsthand the power of servant leadership, though at the time, I didn't think of it as leadership—she was "just a teacher" who cared deeply.

The Legacy of Leadership

One of my most vivid memories of my mother's impact happened years later. While traveling in Washington, D.C., we were walking through Union Station when a former student saw her from a distance. She came running down the stairs, calling out, "Ms. Rector! Ms. Rector!" My mother turned, immediately recognizing her, and called her by name—even though this student had graduated over a decade prior. My mom taught hundreds of students every year at a large Texas high school, yet she made each one feel seen, valued, and remembered.

She wasn't just a teacher—she was a leader. She also held another title in our community: The Welcome Wagon Lady. She was the person who welcomed every new family to town, visiting them, bringing small gifts, and serving as their point of contact for any questions about the area. She made connections everywhere she went. Her ability to listen, communicate, and build relationships shaped not just her career but also my perspective on leadership.

(Welcome Wagon Graduation, 1977)

My mother was a single mom raising two daughters, and while my parents were no longer married, my father remained present in our lives. She mentored my sister and me just as she did her students, encouraging us to speak professionally, get involved, make memories, and step outside our comfort zones. Thanks to her guidance, I became involved in organizations, learned how to lead meetings, understood team dynamics, and brought people together. She was my first and most influential mentor, always checking in, asking thought-provoking questions, and challenging me to become better.

Loss, Reflection, and a New Purpose

In August 2001, my world changed forever. My mother was driving late at night when she fell asleep at the wheel. She was not wearing her seatbelt and was ejected from the vehicle in a fatal single-car accident. I was 27 years old and had just started my first teaching job three days earlier. I had received flowers from her, congratulating me, yet in the chaos of starting a new position, I never got the chance to call her back. I never would.

Losing my mother left a devastating void. I had just married three years prior, finished my master's degree, and was stepping into my teaching career—a journey she had always encouraged me to take. She had always said, "You'll go on to get your doctorate one day," but suddenly, my guide and mentor was gone. I felt lost, questioning why someone so selfless, kind, and impactful would be taken so soon. She was only 61 years old.

Then, just a few weeks later, September 11, 2001, happened. The world was in shock. The United States was under attack, and suddenly, I had clarity.

My mother had spent her life welcoming and guiding others. She had been the Welcome Wagon Lady in our community. In that moment, I realized something profound—God needed her to be the Welcome Wagon Lady in heaven. With the tragic loss of thousands of lives on 9/11, I found peace in believing that my mother had a greater purpose beyond what I could see. That realization changed everything.

We remember those lost and honor their memory today, forever.

UNKNOWN AUTHOR

Carrying the Torch Forward

From that moment, I knew it was my turn to step up. My mother had shown me the way—now, I needed to find my own path. But without her, I needed mentors, guides, and role models to help me navigate leadership.

At first, I turned to famous leadership figures—Tony Robbins, John Maxwell, and other well-known voices in leadership. But something was missing. They focused on theories and aggressive strategies, on "having to do this" and "having to do that." I wanted something deeper, something that blended accountability with empathy and action with service. So, I chose to do what my mother would do—lead by example, mentor others, and serve in a way that elevated those around me.

Over the years, I gained experience in K-12 education, higher education, athletic training, teaching, and administration. I learned the importance of leading not by walking over others, but by walking alongside them. And that is why I created this book—to help support others on their leadership journey.

Inspired by my mother—a remarkable leader in her own right—I embarked on a mission to encourage women to embrace their passion, lead with authenticity, and develop confidence in their abilities. Leadership is not about seeking the spotlight, it is about serving others, supporting them, and helping them grow.

This book is my way of passing on those lessons—to help others step up, step forward, and step into leadership with confidence. It is written in a weekly journal format to encourage reflection, growth, and action. If you are ready to lead with purpose, this book will help you transform your experiences into strength. Let's take this journey together.

Why Am I Writing This in 52 Weeks?

Leadership is a journey, not a race. I've designed this book as a structured, step-by-step guide to help you develop your leadership skills intentionally and sustainably. By breaking it down into weekly lessons, this process becomes manageable, motivating, and effective. You'll be able to track your progress, reflect on your growth, and apply what you learn in real time. While you can move at your own pace, I encourage you to follow the sequence as designed—each step builds upon the last, and skipping ahead may cause you to miss valuable lessons. Take the time to engage fully with each activity, answer every question honestly, and ensure that your responses reflect your own thoughts—not those of your team, supervisor, or anyone else. Leadership is about being authentically you.

One of my favorite leadership reminders is to "wear your own shoes." You can learn from those around you, but at the end of the day, only you can walk your leadership journey. Becoming a strong, confident leader does not happen overnight, it requires time, experience, and reflection. Just as it takes a full year to go through an entire educational cycle, leadership growth follows a similar rhythm. This journey is about embracing the process, learning from challenges, and stepping confidently into the leader you are meant to be. By committing to these weekly lessons, you will exponentially elevate your leadership impact, gaining the skills, mindset, and confidence needed to lead with authenticity and purpose.

How Do You Use This Book?

- Three Sections, Each Section Includes Three Steps, for a total of Nine Steps: This book is built around The Leadership Dance, a framework designed to guide you through key aspects of leadership development.
- Each Month Covers One Step: The Leadership Dance spans nine months (36 weeks), with the remaining weeks dedicated to celebration, reflection, goal setting, and implementation.
- Each Step Is Broken Into Four Weeks: Every week includes a mini lesson, an action step, a motivational quote, and a journal entry to help you apply what you learn.

I encourage you to fully engage with each step. Reflection is not just about analyzing mistakes or difficult experiences; it is a powerful tool for learning, growing, and recognizing opportunities. Your responses may evolve over time, and that's okay. Feel free to revisit and refine your answers as you gain new insights. This journey is about you—your growth, your leadership, and your impact.

The Leadership Dance Framework

- Reflect: Strengthen your self-awareness, purpose, and vision (*Step Up, Step In, Step Out*).
- Strengthen: Build resilience, integrate self-care, and develop meaningful connections (*Step Back, Step Away, Step Across*).
- Elevate: Lead with empowerment and action by navigating challenges, fostering teamwork, and inspiring others (*Step Aside, Step Together, Step Forward*).

Work through each step intentionally and authentically. Many people assume that my leadership journey has been smooth, but the truth is, it has been filled with challenges, setbacks, and growth opportunities. The mindset shift that allowed me to turn obstacles into stepping stones did not happen overnight.

Long ago, I mentioned my mother's influence on my leadership journey. She always encouraged me to see opportunities rather than problems, bridge gaps rather than focus on division, and shift my perspective to create solutions. Because of that, I learned to see challenges as invitations to grow.

Now, as we embark on this journey together, I want you to remember that you are unique. While I can share experiences, lessons, and insights, this book is about helping you develop your own positively authentic leadership style. Wear your own shoes. Don't try to imitate someone else's leadership—instead, take inspiration, gather insights, and craft a leadership approach that is true to who you are.

Are you ready to dance?

The Leadership Dance

Step Out
Step In
Step Up
Reflect
Step Back
Step Away
Strengthen
Step Across
Step Forward
Step Together
Elevate
Step Aside

Do Good
LEADERSHIP

The Leadership Dance

Reflect

Step Up:
Shift

Step In:
Purpose

Step Out:
Vision

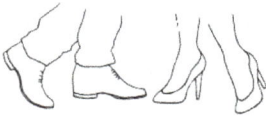

Do Good
LEADERSHIP

SECTION ONE: REFLECT

Shifting from Self-Serving to Selfless Leadership

Leadership begins with reflection. Before we can elevate others, inspire change, or lead with impact, we must first understand ourselves—our motivations, strengths, and areas for growth. In Section One: Reflect, we shift from self-serving leadership to selfless leadership, developing the self-awareness necessary to align our leadership with a greater purpose.

Action

Mindset

Do Good

Mindset Focus: Developing Self-Awareness for Purposeful Leadership

Effective leadership requires intentional reflection—pausing to examine past experiences, analyzing our motivations, and embracing feedback. This phase is about shifting from a leadership style that focuses on personal gain to one that prioritizes service, growth, and impact. True leadership isn't about authority or recognition; it's about how well you support, guide, and empower others.

A self-aware leader is open to feedback and change, stepping outside of their comfort zone to challenge assumptions and ask tough questions. By cultivating self-awareness, leaders gain clarity on their values, passions, and skills, allowing them to lead authentically and with greater purpose.

Action: Committing to Personal Growth and Purposeful Leadership

Throughout this section, we will take an intentional approach to self-reflection, self-discovery, and purposeful leadership. This begins with:

1. Step Up – The Mirror of Leadership: Shifting from Self to Service Leadership is not just about what you do—it's about why you do it. Using the Leadership Grid on an XY Axis Framework, we will analyze the spectrum of self-serving vs. selfless leadership and good vs. bad leadership, identifying where we currently stand and how we can shift toward greater service and impact. Leadership is about inspiring and guiding others, not just personal success.

2. Step In – Aligning Passion with Purpose
    Passion fuels leadership, but purpose gives it direction. Through the Passion Principle Venn Diagram, we will examine how passion, skills, and values intersect to create true purpose. By aligning what we love with what we excel at and what we value most, we ensure that our leadership is meaningful, fulfilling, and sustainable.

3. Step Out – Leading with Vision, Growing with Purpose
    Vision is the driving force behind leadership success. Without it, we remain stagnant—trapped in uncertainty, fear, or inaction. Using the Clarity Cultivates Calculated Choices Framework, we will transition through:

    - Undefined Vision (Comfort Zone)
    - Clarifying Vision (Fear Zone)
    - Vision Refinement (Learning Zone)
    - Vision Execution (Growth Zone)

Additionally, we will explore how our brains reinforce vision clarity through concepts like the Zeigarnik Effect (unfinished tasks stay top-of-mind) and the Baader-Meinhof Phenomenon (we notice what we focus on). By making our vision visible—through vision boards, goal setting, and continuous reflection, we accelerate our leadership progress and impact.

Looking Ahead

As we reflect, align, and refine our leadership approach, we lay the foundation for sustainable growth. By stepping up to selfless leadership, stepping in to align passion with purpose, and stepping out to lead with vision, we begin the journey toward authentic, purpose-driven leadership that elevates both ourselves and those we serve.

The Power of Connection: Choosing How You Lead

Let me share a story with you. When I was in seventh grade, I had a teacher—we'll call her Mrs. Thorne. Mrs. Thorne was horrible. She was petite, with tightly pulled-back blonde hair, thick round glasses, and a scowl that never seemed to leave her face. She always wore the same light-colored knee-length skirt suit, and each day, she would sit down next to the overhead projector, tapping her pen impatiently on the glass as we entered the room. There was no "Hello," no "Welcome to class"—just silence. She gave us exactly three minutes to settle in, and then, without so much as a glance at us, she would say, "Okay, let's go."

Her class was robotic. She would write a math problem on the overhead, walk through the solution, and then say, "Does everybody have it? Good." But she didn't really want an answer—before anyone could respond, she had already erased the problem and moved on. There was no interaction, no discussion, no encouragement. By the time class ended, every single student felt defeated and deflated. I dreaded going. Eventually, I begged my mother, who was a teacher at a nearby high school, to let me switch classes. After some discussion with the principal, I was granted permission to move.

On my first day in my new class, I nervously walked into Mrs. Bloom's classroom, unsure of what to expect. To my surprise, Mrs. Bloom was outside waiting for me. She smiled warmly, welcomed me by name, and guided me to my seat, where a piece of paper sat on my desk. It read, *"Welcome to our class!"*—signed by every single student. She made sure I had all my materials and was ready to learn. When class started, she introduced me to my peers, walked us through the lesson, asked thoughtful questions, encouraged different approaches to problem-solving, and genuinely engaged with us. When class ended, she thanked us for our effort and told us she looked forward to seeing us tomorrow.

The Leadership Choice: Mrs. Thorne or Mrs. Bloom?

Here's the thing—Mrs. Thorne's and Mrs. Bloom's classrooms were identical in many ways. Same school. Same subject. Same curriculum. Same hallway—just three doors apart. So, what made them so drastically different? The way they made their students feel.

Look at the picture of the rose garden. What do you see? Some will notice the vibrant colors, the beautiful flowers, and the sweet fragrance—their positive perspective allows them to appreciate the beauty. Others will focus on the thorns, the bees, the pollen that triggers allergies, and their negative perspective leads them to discomfort.

Your interactions with people are just like this rose garden. Every single day, you have a choice. You can choose to be Mrs. Thorne, remembered for coldness, harsh words, and painful interactions— like thorns, bees, and allergens. Or, you can choose to be Mrs. Bloom, remembered for warmth, kindness, encouragement, and empowerment—like the vibrant flowers, fresh air, and colorful beauty of the garden.

I have found that every interaction in life is like my experience in a seventh-grade math class. You decide whether you bring positivity, encouragement, and connection—or whether you create distance, negativity, and discouragement. Leadership is a choice. You can choose to inspire, uplift, and empower those around you. Let's begin this journey together—to be the leader who leads with authenticity, connection, and care.

STEP 1:
Step Up
Shift

Do Good
LEADERSHIP

Month 1 – Step Up:
Shift from Self-Serving to Selfless Leadership

The first step in your leadership journey is to Step Up—a shift from self-serving leadership to selfless leadership. True leadership is not about authority or accolades; it is about service, impact, and the ability to inspire and elevate others. This month focuses on building a solid foundation in self-awareness, confidence, and purpose. Before leading others, you must first lead yourself with clarity, integrity, and intention. By committing to personal growth, self-awareness, and the leadership mindset, you will develop the foundation necessary to create a meaningful impact.

You will begin by exploring Week 1: The Call to Lead, which challenges you to view leadership as a service-oriented responsibility rather than a position of power. In Week 2: Overcoming Fear, you will confront the doubts and uncertainties that may hold you back, learning to lead with confidence by embracing your unique strengths. Week 3: Leading with Purpose will help you define your personal "Why"—the driving force behind your leadership journey. Finally, in Week 4: Growth Mindset, you will learn how to transform obstacles into opportunities, reframing challenges as stepping stones for success.

By the end of this month, you will have built a strong internal foundation to lead with purpose, courage, and a service-driven mindset. Leadership begins with self-discovery, and this month will equip you with the clarity, confidence, and conviction to step into your role as an empowered, selfless leader. Now, it's time to Step Up and embrace the leader you are meant to be!

Week 1: The Call to Lead – Understanding Leadership as Service

Mini Lesson: The mindset shifts from self-centered to servant leadership

Leadership is not about authority, titles, or recognition—it is about service. True leadership requires a mindset shift from self-serving to servant leadership—from seeking personal gain to empowering and elevating others. Unfortunately, many individuals attain leadership positions and believe they have "made it." They assume leadership is about commanding respect rather than earning trust and inspiring others. This is not leadership; it is dictatorship. Servant leadership is the opposite—it is about prioritizing the needs, growth, and well-being of those you lead.

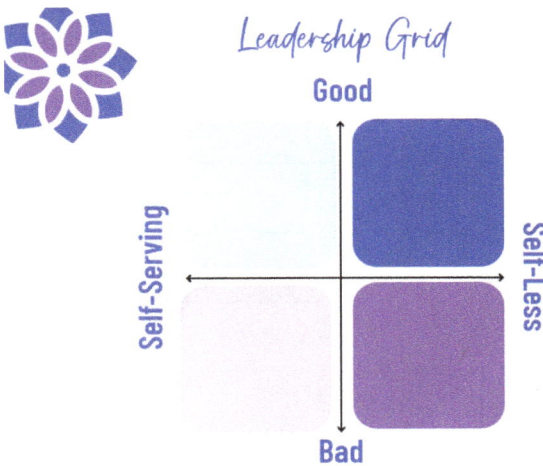

To fully embrace this shift, you must first reevaluate your definition of leadership. Leadership can be good or bad, self-serving, or selfless. Some leaders may be good people but ineffective leaders, while

others may be strong leaders but lack ethical integrity. This is where the Leadership Grid comes in. Take a moment to assess where you currently fall—are you self-serving, leading for recognition and personal validation? Or are you selfless, committed to creating opportunities for those around you? The power lies in your hands. If you do not like where you stand, you can change it. Servant leadership is a choice, an intentional act of putting people first, inspiring growth, and leading with integrity. Starting today, commit to leading with purpose and service.

Action Step: Identify a moment where you lead with service.

_____

_____

_____

_____

_____

_____

_____

_____

_____

_____

_____

_____

"The function of leadership is to produce more leaders, not more followers."

—Ralph Nader

Journal Entry: How can you shift from leading for recognition to leading for impact?

_____

_____

_____

_____

_____

_____

_____

_____

_____

_____

_____

_____

_____

_____

_____

_____

Week 2: Overcoming Fear – Confidence in Your Unique Strengths

Mini Lesson: Recognizing fear as a natural response and learning to lead despite it.

Fear is a natural and instinctive response to the unknown. As humans, we tend to gravitate toward comfort and familiarity—whether in our routines, workplaces, or leadership roles. In education and leadership, we become comfortable with our schedules, curriculum, processes, and even our challenges. However, when a new opportunity arises—one that pushes us outside of this comfort zone, fear often takes hold. Instead of embracing change as an opportunity for growth, we retreat into what feels safe. But here's the truth: Fear is simply a mindset. It is the anticipation of an unknown future, something that has not even happened yet. If we let fear dictate our choices, we will remain stagnant, unable to grow into the leaders we are meant to be.

Shift the Fear

Freeze	**F**	Focus
Evade	**E**	Engage
Avoid	**A**	Act
Retreat	**R**	Rise

To reframe fear, we must shift our perspective. Instead of allowing fear to make us Freeze, Evade, Avoid, and Retreat (F.E.A.R.), we must Focus, Engage, Act, and Rise (F.E.A.R.). The next time fear creeps in, stop and ask yourself: *What if this is an opportunity instead of an obstacle?* What could this experience teach you? How could stepping forward change the course of your leadership journey? One of the best ways to build confidence and overcome fear is to know your strengths. If you have never taken the Clifton StrengthsFinder assessment, consider doing so. Understanding your strengths allows you to see how they have shaped your decisions, career, and relationships—and when you lean into them, your confidence grows. Fear does not disappear; rather, you learn to lead through it with purpose, courage, and self-assurance.

Action Step: Identify and challenge a leadership fear holding you back. Be honest with yourself, what is stopping you from stepping up?

_____

_____

_____

_____

_____

_____

_____

_____

"Fear is only as deep as the mind allows."
—Japanese Proverb

Journal Entry: Write about a time you overcame fear in leadership. What did you learn from the experience? If you cannot think of an example from leadership, reflect on a time in life when you faced a challenge or took a risk despite fear. Every experience is an opportunity to learn. Every experience is a lesson.

_____

_____

_____

_____

_____

_____

_____

_____

_____

_____

_____

_____

_____

_____

_____

_____

Week 3:
Leading with Purpose – Defining Your "Why"

Mini Lesson: Understanding the importance of purpose in leadership.

This week's lesson focuses on the critical role of purpose in leadership. Leadership without purpose is like setting sail without a destination—you may move forward, but you risk drifting aimlessly. A keen sense of "why" provides direction, fuels motivation, and ensures that every decision aligns with your values and long-term vision.

So, what is your "why"? Is it the opportunity to serve and uplift others? Is it about using your platform to empower and guide those around you? Or is it tied to external factors, such as a higher salary, prestigious title, or additional benefits? Understanding your motivation is crucial because your "why" shapes your leadership journey.

Do Good
LEADERSHIP

Align *passion*
with *purpose*
through *introspection*

Take time to reflect on your true purpose. Through introspection, explore what drives you, excites you, and gives you fulfillment. When passion and purpose align, leadership becomes more than just a role—it becomes a mission that sustains and energizes you through challenges and successes.

Action Step: Define your personal leadership purpose statement. This is just your first draft—we will refine it further next month.

_____

_____

_____

_____

_____

_____

_____

_____

_____

_____

_____

_____

_____

_____

_____

"Efforts and courage are not enough without purpose and direction."
—John F. Kennedy

Journal Entry: How does your purpose influence your leadership decisions? If you are unsure about your own leadership, reflect on the leaders around you. Observe their decisions—do they align with their stated purpose? You may be surprised at what you learn.

_____

_____

_____

_____

_____

_____

_____

_____

_____

_____

_____

_____

_____

_____

_____

_____

_____

Week 4: Growth Mindset – Shifting Your Focus to Transform Obstacles Into Opportunities

> ***Mini Lesson:*** The power of continuous learning and adaptability.

A growth mindset is the foundation of resilient and impactful leadership. Dr. Carol Dweck introduced the concept of the growth mindset, which emphasizes that intelligence and abilities can develop through effort, learning, and persistence. Similarly, Angela Duckworth's research on grit highlights the power of perseverance in overcoming challenges. If you haven't read their work, I encourage you to do so—these insights will shift the way you approach obstacles and opportunities.

Far too often, individuals shut down at the first sign of difficulty. A growth mindset flips this narrative. Instead of seeing challenges as roadblocks, see them as opportunities—a chance to rethink, rework, and refine your approach. This ability to adapt and learn continuously is what differentiates leaders who thrive from those who remain stuck.

One way to train yourself in this mindset is to embrace continuous learning. Education is shifting from teacher-centered learning (where knowledge is simply delivered) to learner-centered and holistic education (where individuals actively engage in shaping their learning experience). This same concept applies to leadership. You must be willing to learn, evolve, and adjust—just like adaptive learning programs that tailor lessons based on a student's needs, leadership requires continuous feedback, growth, and strategic shifts.

Continuum of Education
THEN-NOW-NEXT

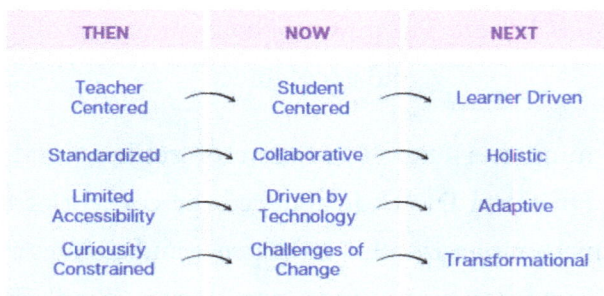

THEN		NOW		NEXT
Teacher Centered		Student Centered		Learner Driven
Standardized		Collaborative		Holistic
Limited Accessibility		Driven by Technology		Adaptive
Curiousity Constrained		Challenges of Change		Transformational

Do Good
LEADERSHIP

If something isn't working, don't quit—adapt. If you struggle in an area, invest in learning and development. Every challenge presents an opportunity, but it is up to you to recognize it and use it to grow.

Action Step: Identify a past failure and reflect on its lesson. Think about a time you faced a challenge. What did you learn? How did it shape you as a leader? Remember, failure is often our greatest teacher.

_____

_____

_____

_____

_____

_____

"Do not be embarrassed by your failures, learn from them and start again."

—Richard Branson

Journal Entry: What challenge can you turn into an opportunity? Consider an area in your leadership journey where you once felt stuck. How can you reframe that experience to fuel your growth and success?

_____

_____

_____

_____

_____

_____

_____

_____

_____

_____

_____

_____

_____

_____

_____

_____

_____

The Leadership Dance

Reflect

STEP 2:

Step In
Purpose

Do Good
LEADERSHIP

Month 2 – Step In:
Find Your Purpose – Aligning Passion with Leadership Impact

Leadership is not just about holding a position, it is about leading with integrity, passion, and authenticity. This month is about stepping in—fully committing to who you are as a leader and ensuring that your actions align with your values and purpose. One of the greatest challenges leaders face is feeling stuck—unsure of their next step or whether they are even on the right path. But what if those moments of uncertainty were opportunities for self-discovery, alignment, and growth? The key is reframing challenges into lessons that help us define our core values, align our skills with our passions, and lead authentically.

Throughout this month, you will explore the foundational aspects of leadership identity. Week 5 focuses on identifying core values, the internal compass that guides every decision and interaction. Without clear values, leadership can become misaligned and directionless. Week 6 dives into the balance between passion and skill, helping you recognize where your strengths and enthusiasm intersect so that you can maximize your leadership impact. Week 7 challenges you to lead authentically, embracing who you are instead of trying to fit into a predefined mold of leadership. Finally, Week 8 is about saying yes to purpose—overcoming self-doubt, trusting your leadership journey, and stepping forward with confidence.

If you have ever felt uncertain, stuck, or questioned your leadership path, this is the month to turn that doubt into direction. By aligning with your values, understanding your unique strengths, and committing to authenticity, you will step into leadership with clarity and purpose—ready to overcome challenges, fuel growth, and lead with impact.

Week 5: Identifying Core Values – Your Leadership Compass

> ***Mini Lesson:*** Understanding the role of core values in decision-making.

Your core values serve as your leadership compass, guiding every decision, interaction, and response. When your leadership aligns with your values, you become an authentic and intentional leader, capable of making clear and confident decisions. However, when your values and leadership approach are misaligned, you may feel unfulfilled, disconnected, or even compromised in your role. That is why it is essential to identify, clarify, and commit to the values that shape your leadership identity.

As you reflect on your core values, consider the ethical framework that guides you. Do you prioritize honesty, integrity, accountability, or service? Are your values centered on growth, collaboration, or innovation? Your core values influence how you lead, how you interact with others, and how you navigate challenges. In some cases, you may find yourself in an organization where your values align seamlessly—creating a fulfilling and purpose-driven leadership experience. In other cases, you may realize that your values clash with the culture or expectations of your workplace, signaling a potential misalignment. Identifying your ethical framework early ensures that you can make intentional decisions about where and how you lead.

Activity: Ethical Framework

- In this activity, we will use a visual XY axis to help you create a personal ethical framework that aligns with professional standards focused on integrity.

- Each quadrant of the axis represents a different area in the life of an educator, guiding you to reflect on various aspects of your ethical values and commitments.

- **Quadrant 1: Core Values**

- **Quadrant 2: Self-Reflection and Growth**

- **Quadrant 3: Interprofessional Collaboration**

- **Quadrant 4: Personal Integrity**

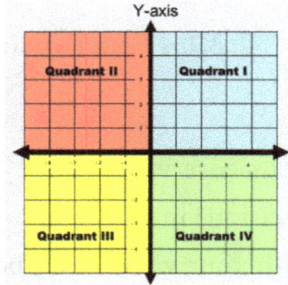

Key Components in Education

- Integrity
- Respect
- Responsibility
- Fairness
- Honesty
- Compassion
- Empathy
- Equity
- Accountability

- Transparency
- Trustworthiness
- Professionalism
- Confidentiality
- Collaboration
- Diversity
- Inclusivity
- Ethical leadership
- Academic integrity

- Authenticity
- Courage
- Advocacy
- Reflection
- Lifelong learning
- Social responsibility
- Critical thinking
- Moral courage
- Balance

For each quadrant, create an action statement related to your personal ethical code.

ACTION: Create Statements

- Starters:
  - I am committed to...
  - I prioritize...
  - I value...
  - I strive to...
  - I uphold...

- I believe in...
- I advocate for...
- I promote...
- I embrace...
- I exemplify...
- I integrate...

Sample Personal Ethical Framework

1. Core Values:

- Integrity: I commit to upholding honesty, transparency, and consistency in all my actions and decisions.

- Respect: I recognize and honor the inherent worth and dignity of every individual, fostering a classroom environment where all voices are valued and heard.

- Compassion: I approach interactions with empathy and kindness, understanding the unique challenges and experiences of each student.

- Lifelong Learning: I believe in the pursuit of knowledge and continuous personal and professional growth, as well as modeling curiosity and intellectual curiosity for my students.

2. Self-Reflection and Growth:

- Reflection: I regularly engage in self-reflection to examine my beliefs, biases, and assumptions, seeking opportunities for personal and professional growth.

- Adaptability: I embrace feedback and constructive criticism as opportunities for learning and improvement, remaining open-minded and flexible in my approach to teaching.

- Emotional Intelligence: I strive to understand and manage my emotions effectively, recognizing their impact on my interactions with students and colleagues.

- Growth Mindset: I cultivate a growth mindset in myself and my students, fostering resilience, perseverance, and a willingness to embrace challenges as learning opportunities.

Sample Personal Ethical Framework

3. Interprofessional Collaboration:

- Collaboration: I value collaboration and teamwork, actively seeking opportunities to collaborate with colleagues, parents, and community stakeholders to support student success.

- Communication: I prioritize clear and effective communication, fostering open dialogue and mutual respect in all collaborative endeavors.

- Shared Goals: I work collaboratively to establish shared goals and objectives, recognizing the importance of collective efforts in achieving positive outcomes for students.

- Professional Development: I engage in collaborative professional development activities, sharing knowledge, expertise, and best practices with colleagues to enhance our collective impact.

4. Personal Integrity:

- Accountability: I take responsibility for my actions and decisions, holding myself to the highest ethical standards and accountability.

- Authenticity: I strive to align my actions with my values, maintaining authenticity and consistency in my interactions and relationships.

- Ethical Leadership: I lead by example, demonstrating integrity, fairness, and ethical behavior in all aspects of my role as an educator.

- Trustworthiness: I build and maintain trust with students, colleagues, and the community through transparency, reliability, and ethical conduct

Action Step: Create your ethical framework.

_____

_____

_____

_____

_____

"When your values are clear, your decisions are easy."

—Roy Disney

Journal Entry: Reflect on a past leadership decision and how your values influenced it.

If you have not been in a formal leadership position, think about decisions made by leaders in your life. Did their actions align with their core values? What did you learn from observing their leadership?

_____

_____

_____

_____

_____

_____

_____

_____

_____

_____

_____

_____

_____

_____

_____

_____

Week 6: Passion vs. Skill – Aligning Your Gifts

Mini Lesson: Recognizing the intersection of passion and skill in leadership.

Many people believe their purpose is something separate from what they love, but true fulfillment in leadership comes when passion, skills, and values align. When you lead with passion, your purpose flows naturally. Understanding how your strengths, interests, and values intersect will help you make intentional leadership decisions that feel both authentic and impactful.

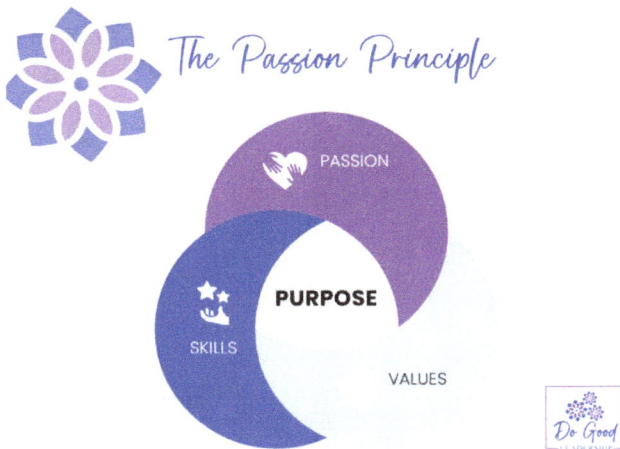

Let's take a closer look at these key components:

- Passion: What excites and energizes you? Passion is what makes your heart race in an effective way and gives meaning to your work. It's what you could talk about for hours without getting tired.

- Skills: What are your natural talents? Skills include both developed abilities and natural strengths that make you stand out. These are the things you excel at and enjoy doing.
- Values: What are your guiding principles? Values shape how you make decisions, interact with others, and approach challenges. They form the ethical foundation of your leadership.
- Purpose: Where passion, skills, and values converge, you find your purpose. Purpose isn't just about what you do—it's about finding meaning in your work that aligns with who you are and what you stand for.

When you align these three elements, leadership becomes more than a role; it becomes a calling. You feel fulfilled, energized, and motivated to make a lasting impact.

Action Step: Identify one area where your passion and skills align. Does it match what you are doing today?

_____

_____

_____

_____

_____

_____

_____

_____

"Passion is energy.
Feel the power that comes from focusing
on what excites you."
—Oprah Winfrey

Journal Entry: How can you incorporate more passion into your leadership style?

(Authenticity plays a huge role in this. When you lead with authenticity, your passion becomes evident to those around you. If you are inauthentic, people will sense the lack of passion, and it will resonate loudly. How can you ensure that your leadership is driven by your true passions?)

_____

_____

_____

_____

_____

_____

_____

_____

_____

_____

_____

_____

_____

_____

_____

Week 7: Leading Authentically – The Power of Being Yourself

> *Mini Lesson:* The impact of authenticity on leadership.

Too often, leaders put on a mask, presenting one version of themselves at work and another in their personal lives. This disconnect between who they are and how they lead creates a lack of trust among their team. Authentic leaders, however, don't change based on their environment—they remain genuine, consistent, and true to their values.

Authenticity in leadership is about alignment—aligning what you say, what you do, and who you are. People respect leaders who follow through on their promises, lead by example, and treat others with integrity. When leaders are authentic, it creates a culture of trust and loyalty. Employees, students, or teams will be more willing to follow a leader who is real, honest, and transparent rather than one who only seeks to impress, dictate, or control.

Ask yourself:

- Do you practice what you preach?
- Do you treat people with the same respect, regardless of their position?

- Do you lead in a way that reflects your personal values?

Authenticity isn't about being perfect, it's about being real. The more authentic you are, the stronger your influence, the deeper your connections, and the greater your impact.

Action Step: Identify a leadership trait that makes you unique. What makes you stand out from everybody else?

_____

_____

_____

_____

_____

_____

_____

_____

_____

_____

_____

_____

_____

_____

_____

"Authenticity is a collection of choices that we have to make every day."

—Brené Brown

Journal Entry: When have you led authentically, and what was the impact?

(If you are new to leadership, think about a time when you influenced or guided someone in a meaningful way. If you are a teacher, you are already a leader in your classroom. Authentic leadership happens in all areas of life. Reflect on an experience where you stayed true to yourself, and it made a difference.)

_____

_____

_____

_____

_____

_____

_____

_____

_____

_____

_____

_____

_____

_____

Week 8: Saying Yes to Purpose – Overcoming Doubt

Mini Lesson: Embracing self-belief and stepping into purpose.

One of the biggest barriers to leadership growth is self-doubt. Often, we are our own worst critics, questioning our abilities even when others see our potential. Although we may have a clear purpose, we hesitate to fully step into it. This hesitation can come from fear of failure, a lack of confidence, or simply feeling unworthy of success. But true leaders recognize their self-worth and choose to believe in themselves before anyone else does.

Mel Robbins, a renowned motivational speaker, emphasizes the power of self-encouragement in her book *The High Five Habit*. She explains that while we freely support and celebrate others, we rarely offer ourselves the same encouragement. Her simple yet powerful technique—giving yourself a high-five in the mirror each morning—can create a positive mindset shift. It may feel awkward at first, but with consistency, it helps build self-belief, motivation, and resilience. Try it! Stand in front of the mirror, look yourself in the eye, and give yourself that high-five. The act alone releases dopamine and starts your day with a moment of self-celebration.

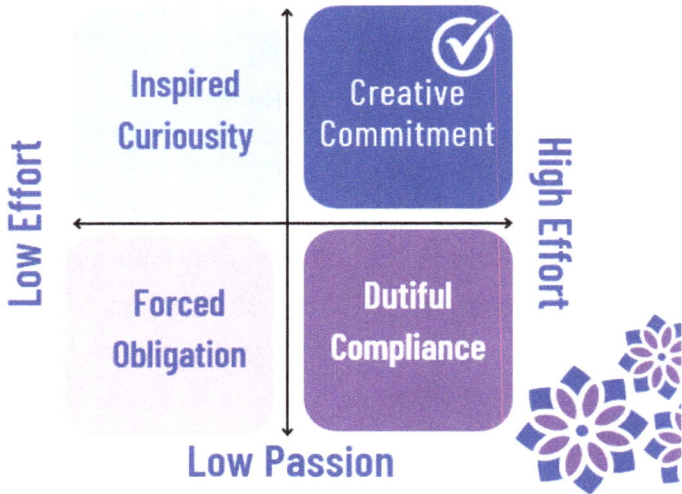

Passion Drives Effort Matrix

High Passion

Low Effort / **High Effort**

Inspired Curiousity

Creative Commitment

Forced Obligation

Dutiful Compliance

Low Passion

Finding Purpose: The Passion Drives Effort Matrix

When we embrace our purpose, we also see a natural increase in our effort and motivation. The Passion Drives Effort Matrix helps illustrate how our level of passion and effort impact our work:

1. Low Passion, Low Effort (*Forced Obligation*)
   - Feeling unmotivated and disengaged, leading to low productivity.

2. High Effort, Low Passion (*Dutiful Compliance*)
   - Putting in hard work but lacking true enthusiasm, often out of obligation.

3. High Passion, Low Effort (*Inspired Curiosity*)
   - Excited and interested, but not fully committed to action.

4. High Passion, High Effort (*Creative Commitment*)
   - Fully engaged, motivated, and dedicated, resulting in true fulfillment and success.

Are you operating in the Creative Commitment quadrant? If not, what needs to change? What shifts do you need to make to fully align passion with effort?

Action Step: Write a letter to yourself affirming your leadership journey. Reflect on your wins, achievements, and growth. Read this letter aloud to yourself as if you were encouraging a friend.

_____

_____

_____

_____

_____

_____

_____

_____

_____

_____

_____

_____

_____

"Doubt kills more dreams than failure ever will."

—Suzy Kassem

Journal Entry: What doubts do you need to release to fully embrace your leadership?

_____

_____

_____

_____

_____

_____

_____

_____

_____

_____

_____

_____

_____

_____

_____

_____

_____

_____

STEP 3:
Step Out
Vision

Do Good
LEADERSHIP

Month 3 – Step Out:
Create Your Vision Through Purpose

Leading with intentionality and clarity. Stepping out as a leader means creating a vision through your purpose—ensuring that every action, decision, and goal aligns with your long-term aspirations. Leadership is not just about reacting to the present but also about intentionally shaping the future. To do this effectively, you need to balance both perspectives: the microscope and the telescope.

The microscope represents your daily focus—the tasks, decisions, and interactions that demand your immediate attention. These small but essential actions shape your leadership impact. However, if you only focus on short-term tasks, you risk losing sight of your bigger purpose. The telescope, on the other hand, represents your long-term vision—the leadership legacy you want to create, the impact you want to leave behind, and the personal and professional growth you aim to achieve. True leadership requires balancing both perspectives, ensuring that your daily efforts contribute to your greater purpose.

This month focuses on navigating change, stepping outside of comfort zones, and effectively communicating your vision. Leaders must be able to adapt with confidence when faced with uncertainty, embrace discomfort to challenge themselves and grow, and articulate their vision clearly so that others can align with and support their mission.

A Lesson in Vision: Grace's Story

I once mentored a remarkable woman named Grace, who had immigrated from another country. Despite being well-educated and experienced—having served as a hospital administrator in her home country, she faced constant doubt and discrimination in her new workplace. Because of her accent, colleagues dismissed her intelligence and belittled her contributions. They questioned her abilities, restricted her communication, and even told her that she would never advance in the organization. Over time, Grace absorbed their negativity, allowing it to chip away at her vision and confidence. But once she reconnected with her own value and worth, everything began to shift. Her confidence steadily returned, and with newfound clarity, she began applying for other roles. Within just 30 days, she secured a new position—one where her expertise was recognized, her voice respected, and her presence celebrated.

Grace's story is a powerful reminder of how important it is to protect your vision from external doubts. She had the skills, the knowledge, and the drive—but she allowed others to define her worth. As leaders, we must learn to navigate challenges with confidence and step outside of our comfort zones despite fear and uncertainty. Most importantly, we must communicate our vision clearly, ensuring that others understand, respect, and align with our leadership goals.

Week 9 focuses on crafting your leadership vision, helping you understand the power of having a clear and compelling direction for yourself and those you lead. You'll learn to speak your vision in the present tense and use tools like vision boards to keep your goals front and center. Week 10 explores navigating change with confidence and recognizing that change is an inevitable part of leadership. You'll reflect on where you may be resisting change and discover how to become more adaptable and resilient using the Behavioral Stages of Change framework. Week 11 invites you to embrace the courage to step outside your comfort zone, showing that growth happens when you challenge yourself beyond the familiar. You'll take small, intentional steps to push past fear and build the confidence needed to expand your leadership impact. Week 12 centers on communicating your vision clearly, teaching you how to use storytelling to inspire, engage, and align others with your goals. You'll practice refining your message so it resonates deeply and motivates action in those you lead.

By the end of this month, like Grace, you will have a clearer understanding of your vision, a stronger sense of purpose, and the tools needed to lead with intentionality—balancing the microscope of daily leadership actions with the telescope of your long-term impact. Are you ready to step out and create your vision with purpose?

Week 9: Crafting Your Leadership Vision

> ***Mini Lesson:*** The importance of having a clear and compelling vision.

A clear and compelling vision is the foundation of impactful leadership. Where do you see yourself? Where are you leading others? The way you articulate your vision will determine the direction of your journey. When crafting your leadership vision, speak as if it is already happening—not in the future, but in the present tense. Instead of saying, "I hope to become an influential leader in education," shift your mindset and say, "I am an influential leader in education who empowers others daily." The more vivid and precise your vision, the more focused and intentional you will become in working toward it.

Zeigarnik Effect

Vision boards are an effective tool for reinforcing this clarity. Have you ever noticed that when you start thinking about purchasing something new, whether it's a car, a pair of shoes, or a specific brand, you suddenly start seeing it everywhere? This is called the Zeigarnik effect, a psychological phenomenon where your brain prioritizes unfinished goals and makes you more aware of related opportunities. The same happens when you define and visualize your leadership vision daily. Your mind will seek out ways to make it happen, connecting you with the right people, opportunities, and resources. Take the time to write your leadership vision statement, ensuring that it is specific, detailed, and aligned with your values. This vision will serve as your guiding light in every leadership decision you make.

Action Step: Write a vision statement for your leadership journey. Be as detailed and specific as possible.

_____

_____

_____

_____

_____

_____

_____

_____

_____

_____

_____

_____

"The only thing worse than being blind is having sight but no vision."

—Helen Keller

Journal Entry: How does your vision guide your leadership decisions?

_____

_____

_____

_____

_____

_____

_____

_____

_____

_____

_____

_____

_____

_____

_____

_____

_____

Week 10: Navigating Change with Confidence

> ***Mini Lesson:*** Understanding change as an inevitable part of leadership.

Many of us resist change, clinging to the comfort of familiarity and the belief that if something isn't broken, it doesn't need fixing. The thought of altering a well-established system can feel overwhelming, risky, and even unnecessary. However, leadership is about growth, adaptability, and progress. The reality is, change is constant, and whether we initiate it or it is imposed upon us, we must learn to embrace it with confidence rather than fear.

Behavioral Stages of Change

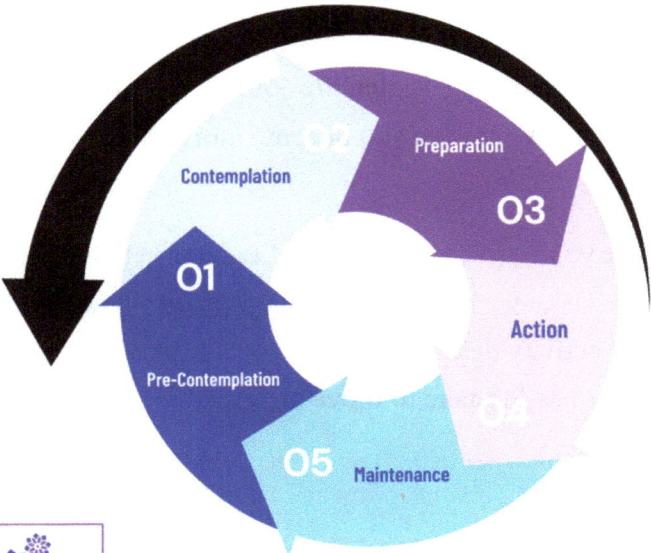

Contemplation

Preparation

O3

O1

Action

Pre-Contemplation

O5 Maintenance

Do Good
LEADERSHIP

To better understand how individuals navigate change, consider the Behavioral Stages of Change framework. Originally developed for health behavior change, this model can be applied to leadership and education. It identifies five distinct stages:

- Pre-Contemplation: Resistance to or avoidance of change.
- Contemplation: Recognizing that change may be necessary, but feeling uncertain or hesitant.
- Preparation: Taking small steps toward change and strategizing how to implement it.
- Action: Actively engaging in the change process.
- Maintenance: Sustaining the change and integrating it into long-term habits.

Unlike personal change decisions, leadership change is often out of our direct control. We must learn to adjust, support, and guide others through transitions. As a leader, you are responsible for fostering a mindset that views change as an opportunity rather than a setback. Where in your leadership journey do you find yourself resisting change? Where can you become more adaptable and open-minded?

To determine your current stage in the Leadership Behavioral Stages of Change, visit www.drstephanieduguid.com/ready-to-lead to download an activity designed to help you assess where you are and what steps you need to take to move forward.

Action Step: Identify one area where you need to be more adaptable.

_____

_____

_____

_____

_____

_____

_____

_____

_____

_____

_____

_____

_____

_____

_____

_____

_____

_____

Quote: *"Change is the law of life. And those who look only to the past or present are certain to miss the future."*
—John F. Kennedy

(That is one of the reasons change is important. If we cling to the status quo, we miss opportunities for growth and transformation.)

Journal Entry: How do you respond to change, and how can you improve?

_____

_____

_____

_____

_____

_____

_____

_____

_____

_____

_____

_____

_____

_____

_____

_____

_____

_____

Week 11: The Courage to Step Outside Comfort Zones

> ***Mini Lesson:*** Growth happens outside your comfort zone.

We have all heard the saying, "Growth happens outside your comfort zone," but what does that truly mean? Imagine your comfort zone as an old, worn-out pair of shoes—comfortable, familiar, but fraying at the edges, with soles that no longer provide support. Even though they no longer serve you well, you hesitate to replace them because change makes you feel uncomfortable. Now, imagine you want to take on a new challenge—a hike up a mountain. Your old shoes aren't suited for the terrain, yet you resist swapping them for something new. By clinging to what's familiar, you risk missing out on incredible opportunities for exploration, learning, and personal growth.

The Climb from Comfort to Capability

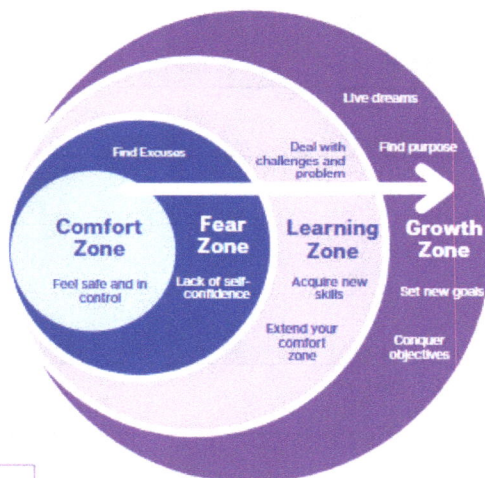

Live dreams

Find Excuses

Deal with challenges and problem

Find purpose

Comfort Zone

Feel safe and in control

Fear Zone

Lack of self-confidence

Learning Zone

Acquire new skills

Growth Zone

Set new goals

Extend your comfort zone

Conquer objectives

Do Good
LEADERSHIP

Leadership works the same way. Staying in your comfort zone may feel safe, but it also limits your potential. When you step into new challenges, whether it's speaking up in meetings, tackling a difficult conversation, or taking on a leadership role, you stretch beyond what you thought was possible. This is where the real transformation happens. Look at the Comfort Zone Growth Model—notice that as soon as you leave your safe space, the first thing you feel is fear. Fear of the unknown, fear of failure, fear of judgment. But the more you push forward, the more you learn, build confidence, and eventually grow into a stronger, more capable leader.

Action Step: Take one leadership action that makes you uncomfortable. It doesn't have to be big—just one small, intentional step outside your comfort zone. For example, if you struggle with initiating conversations, challenge yourself to approach a colleague and say hello. If public speaking is intimidating, volunteer to lead a discussion. Growth begins one step at a time!

_____

_____

_____

_____

_____

_____

_____

"Life begins at the end of your comfort zone."

—Neale Donald Walsch

Journal Entry: Reflect on a time when stepping out of your comfort zone led to growth. What did you learn from that experience? How did it change your perspective on taking risks and embracing challenges?

_____

_____

_____

_____

_____

_____

_____

_____

_____

_____

_____

_____

_____

_____

_____

_____

Week 12: Communicating Vision Clearly

Mini Lesson: The role of storytelling in sharing your vision effectively.

Do Good
LEADERSHIP

Clarity
Cultivates
Calculated
Choices

A leader's ability to communicate their vision clearly is one of the most powerful tools for inspiring action. It's not enough to have a vision; you must be able to articulate it in a way that excites, motivates, and aligns your team. Many leaders struggle with this, delivering their vision in a monotone, memorized way that lacks passion and connection. When vision is unclear or uninspiring, those around you won't buy in or feel motivated to contribute.

However, when you communicate your vision with clarity, enthusiasm, and purpose, others become energized and engaged. Think of great leaders and speakers, they captivate their audience through storytelling. Storytelling makes vision relatable, tangible, and impactful. If you can paint a picture of where you're going, people will want to follow. This is why clarity cultivates calculated choices—when people understand the vision, they can make intentional decisions to support it. Take the time to practice articulating your vision to a colleague, mentor, or trusted friend. Refine your message and ensure it resonates with others. Clear communication is essential for leadership success.

Clarity Cultivates Calculated Choices

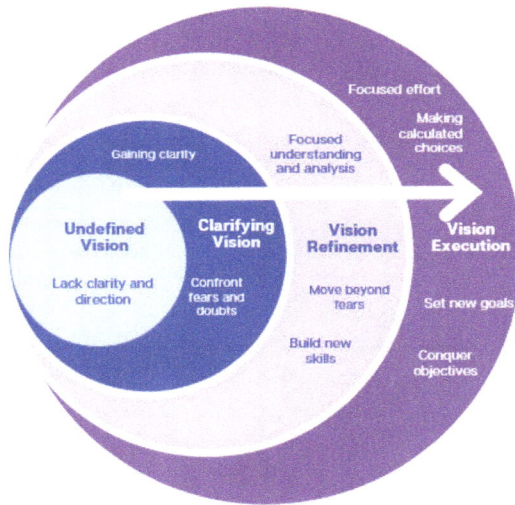

Action Step: Practice articulating your vision to a colleague or mentor. How does it sound? Does it inspire action?

_____

_____

_____

_____

_____

_____

_____

_____

_____

_____

_____

_____

_____

_____

_____

"Great leaders communicate a vision that inspires action."
—John C. Maxwell

Journal Entry: How can you improve how you communicate your vision? If public speaking makes you uncomfortable, start small. Practice with a friend, record yourself, or rehearse in front of a mirror. Developing effective communication skills takes time, but every leader must learn to share their vision effectively.

_____

_____

_____

_____

_____

_____

_____

_____

_____

_____

_____

_____

_____

_____

_____

_____

The Leadership Dance

Strengthen

Step Back: Reinforce

Step Away: Synthesize

Step Across: Connect

Do Good
LEADERSHIP

SECTION TWO: STRENGTHEN

Building Resilience and Strong Relationships to Support Leadership Growth

Leadership is a journey, and as you move from reflection to action, the next critical phase is strengthening—reinforcing the foundation of your leadership through resilience, relationships, and adaptability. Leadership can feel isolating, especially in educational settings where individuals often transition from faculty to administration, shifting from being peers to supervisors. This transition brings challenges— managing expectations, navigating workplace dynamics, and balancing increased responsibilities with personal well-being.

In this phase, we focus on building resilience and strong connections to ensure sustainable leadership. Strengthening requires reinforcing personal and professional foundations, prioritizing self-care, and cultivating meaningful relationships. Without intentional effort, leadership can become overwhelming, leading to burnout and disconnection. The key is not just managing responsibilities but thriving in them—learning to balance duties, maintain well-being, and foster trust-based relationships that support long-term success.

Mindset Focus: Reinforcing Leadership Through Reflection, Resilience, and Relationships

This phase requires a mindset shift—one that embraces continuous improvement and empowerment through learning. Growth doesn't happen overnight, nor does it happen in isolation. Leaders must commit to evolving their methods, embracing challenges, and strengthening their ability to navigate change. Resilient leaders don't just survive difficulties; they adapt, learn, and emerge stronger. Strength also comes from connection. By investing in professional relationships, collaborating with peers, and fostering open communication, leaders build a network of support that sustains them through challenges.

Action: Strengthening Self-Awareness, Adaptability, and Connection

This section focuses on three critical steps to help leaders strengthen their leadership foundation and capacity:

1. Step Back – Reinforce Your Foundation for Success
    *   A leader's strength is rooted in core values and principles. By grounding yourself in a clear leadership philosophy, you create stability, confidence, and adaptability. This step focuses on reflecting on what drives your leadership, ensuring that your foundation is strong enough to support growth and resilience in the face of challenges.

2. Step Away – Synthesize & Prioritize Well-Being
    *   True leadership requires synthesis and integration of work, family, and self-care. Leaders often compartmentalize, trying to keep different areas of life separate, but sustainable leadership requires integration over isolation. In this step, we explore restorative leadership, learning how intentional self-care strengthens resilience, prevents burnout, and fosters longevity in leadership roles.

3. Step Across – Connect & Build Relationships
    *   Leadership is built on communication and connection. The way we speak, listen, and engage with others shapes outcomes, relationships, and workplace culture. Effective communication aligns perspectives, fosters trust, and empowers collaboration. This step focuses on strengthening interpersonal skills, evaluating communication strategies, and building relationships that create a meaningful impact.

Looking Ahead

As you move through Section Two: Strengthen, you will reinforce your foundation, integrate self-care into leadership, and cultivate strong professional relationships. By stepping back, stepping away, and stepping across, you will develop the resilience, adaptability, and connections needed to thrive as a leader. Leadership is not about standing alone, it's about strengthening yourself so you can empower others.

The Leadership Dance
Strengthen

STEP 4:
Step Back
Reinforce

Month 4 – Step Back:
Reinforce Your Foundation

Reassessing and Strengthening Personal and Professional Foundations

Leadership is not just about moving forward; it's also about knowing when to step back, reassess, and reinforce your foundation. A strong leader is not built solely on ambition or drive but on core values, principles, and a clear sense of purpose. While leadership may seem like a forward-moving journey, true growth comes from moments of reflection and recalibration. Challenges, setbacks, and unexpected detours are inevitable, but a leader with a solid foundation remains steady, navigating difficulties with clarity and confidence. Stepping back is not about retreating; it's about strengthening. By taking the time to reflect on past experiences, reassess priorities, and reinforce personal and professional frameworks, leaders ensure they are prepared for long-term success.

Just as a well-constructed building can withstand storms, a leader with a solid foundation can endure adversity without losing focus. This month focuses on the power of reflection, recognizing growth through challenges, and learning to establish boundaries that protect energy and well-being. It begins with examining lessons learned from past experiences, followed by embracing setbacks as opportunities for growth. Leaders will also explore the power of self-awareness and recalibrate their approach, before learning how to establish boundaries and integrate work-life balance without burnout. When leaders take the time to step back and fortify their foundation, they are not only reinforcing their own growth but also strengthening their ability to guide, support, and inspire others.

Week 13 focuses on reflection and lessons learned, helping you understand the value of pausing to look back on your leadership experiences. You'll explore how intentional reflection—both individually and with trusted colleagues—can help you grow, refine your approach, and celebrate your successes, shaping the leader you are becoming. Week 14 explores strength in setbacks and growth from challenges, encouraging you to reframe failures and difficulties as opportunities for resilience and progress. You'll discover how to pivot, adapt, and turn obstacles into stepping stones toward stronger, more effective leadership. Week 15 centers on recalibrating and realigning, reminding you of the importance of integrity and values-based decision-making. You'll reflect on how to adjust your priorities and leadership strategies so that they remain aligned with your core values, ensuring your leadership impact is both ethical and sustainable. Week 16 highlights the importance of boundaries and integration to protect your energy, teaching you how to balance professional responsibilities with personal well-being. You'll learn strategies to set healthy boundaries, avoid burnout, and create a leadership rhythm that supports both your work and your life.

Week 13: Reflection & Lessons Learned

> *Mini Lesson:* Understanding the value of reflection in leadership.

The MORE you REFLECT the MORE you LEARN

Building a strong personal and professional foundation is essential for confidently navigating leadership challenges. Leadership is not just about moving forward, it's also about looking back, learning from experiences, and using those lessons to grow. Reflection is a powerful tool that allows leaders to assess their decisions, recognize patterns, and improve their approach over time. You may have noticed that throughout this journey, we have taken moments to pause and reflect. Now, it's time to make reflection a consistent and intentional habit in your leadership practice.

One of the best ways to cultivate this habit is by maintaining a leadership journal. Set aside five to ten minutes each day to reflect on your experiences, challenges, and accomplishments. This practice is not just about analyzing mistakes but also about celebrating successes and understanding what works well. Reflection can also be a collaborative process, where you engage in conversations with trusted mentors or colleagues to gain valuable insights and constructive feedback. While feedback may sometimes be difficult to hear, true growth happens when leaders embrace the opportunity to adapt, refine, and enhance their leadership strategies.

Action Step: Identify three leadership lessons from past experiences.

_____

_____

_____

_____

_____

_____

_____

_____

_____

_____

_____

_____

_____

_____

_____

"We do not learn from experience... we learn from reflecting on experience."
—John Dewey

Journal Entry: What leadership lessons have shaped who you are today?

_____

_____

_____

_____

_____

_____

_____

_____

_____

_____

_____

_____

_____

_____

_____

_____

_____

_____

Week 14: Strength in Setbacks – Growth from Challenges

> ***Mini Lesson:*** Embracing failures and setbacks as opportunities for growth.

In leadership, setbacks are inevitable. However, how you respond to these challenges defines your growth. You can either view difficulties as insurmountable obstacles that weigh you down, or you can see them as stepping stones toward greater resilience and success. True leadership requires a mindset shift—rather than giving up at the first sign of adversity, you must learn to pivot, adapt, and find new ways to navigate challenges. Every setback carries within it a lesson, an opportunity to refine your approach, develop new skills, and strengthen your leadership.

The journey of leadership is rarely a straight, obstacle-free path. While we often expect smooth progress, reality presents twists and turns—mountains to climb, valleys to cross, and unexpected storms to weather. The difference between leaders who succeed and those who struggle is their ability to embrace these hurdles as part of the process. Rather than seeing failure as an endpoint, view it as a redirection toward a better path. Persistence, creativity, and resourcefulness will turn today's setbacks into tomorrow's breakthroughs. By learning how to reframe challenges as opportunities, you will develop the confidence and resilience needed to lead effectively.

Prepare for Setbacks

Action Step: Identify a past challenge and outline the lessons learned.

_____

_____

_____

_____

_____

_____

_____

_____

_____

_____

_____

_____

"Success is not final; failure is not fatal: it is the courage to continue that counts."

—Winston Churchill

Journal Entry: How can you reframe past challenges to fuel future success?

_____

_____

_____

_____

_____

_____

_____

_____

_____

_____

_____

_____

_____

_____

_____

_____

Week 15: Leading with Integrity – Making Values-Based Decisions

> *Mini Lesson:* The importance of integrity in decision-making.

Integrity is the foundation of strong, values-based leadership. It is more than just following policies and adhering to procedures—it is about making ethical decisions that align with both the expectations of your organization and the well-being of those affected by your choices. Policies provide structure, but true integrity requires balancing those guidelines with fairness, ethical reasoning, and consistency. Every decision you make is part of a larger framework, setting a precedent for future choices and shaping the leadership culture around you. Leaders who prioritize integrity foster trust, create stability, and set a powerful example for those they lead.

Consistency in decision-making is key to building credibility as a leader. Your choices should reflect your core values, past decisions, and the long-term impact of your leadership. When you make decisions with integrity, you establish a culture of trust and accountability. Even when faced with difficult choices or external pressure, standing firm in your principles strengthens your leadership and leaves a lasting, positive impact. True leadership is not about seeking approval, it is about making the right choices even when no one is watching. By leading with integrity, you create a foundation of respect and ethical leadership that extends beyond your immediate influence.

Success Takes Consistency

Action Step: Define your personal leadership values and how they guide your decisions.

_____

_____

_____

_____

_____

_____

_____

_____

_____

_____

"Integrity is doing the right thing, even when no one is watching."

—C. S. Lewis

Journal Entry: Describe a situation where you upheld your integrity as a leader.

_____

_____

_____

_____

_____

_____

_____

_____

_____

_____

_____

_____

_____

_____

_____

_____

Week 16: Boundaries & Integration – Protecting Your Energy

Mini Lesson: Setting healthy boundaries to sustain effective leadership.

Many leaders step into new roles with enthusiasm, eager to serve and make an impact. However, in their drive to meet expectations and fulfill responsibilities, they often neglect their well-being. I've seen this happen time and time again—not only in colleagues but in my own experience. The desire to be a strong, committed leader can lead to overextending yourself, sacrificing rest, neglecting health, and putting personal commitments on the back burner. Over time, this leads to stress, exhaustion, and even burnout. Leadership is not just about serving others, it's about sustaining yourself so you can continue to lead effectively. That's why boundaries and integration are crucial to long-term success.

Protect Your Energy

Setting boundaries does not mean shutting off leadership responsibilities entirely. Instead, it means creating a balance that allows for both professional excellence and personal well-being. A guest on my podcast once shared an insightful perspective—rather than viewing boundaries as a strict division, think of them as a way to blend responsibilities in a way that supports both professional and personal priorities. For example, if an event is required at work, consider involving your family so that it becomes a shared experience rather than a personal sacrifice. Similarly, when personal priorities arise, honor them, knowing that your team and organization will function in your absence. Having a plan in place allows you to set boundaries without guilt, protecting your energy and ensuring that you can lead with strength and sustainability.

Action Step: Identify an area where you need to set stronger boundaries.

_____

_____

_____

_____

_____

_____

_____

_____

"Daring to set boundaries is about having the courage to love ourselves, even when we risk disappointing others."
—Brené Brown

Journal Entry: How can you balance leadership responsibilities while prioritizing self-care?

_____

_____

_____

_____

_____

_____

_____

_____

_____

_____

_____

_____

_____

_____

_____

_____

_____

STEP 5:

Step Away

Synthesize

Do Good
LEADERSHIP

Month 5 – Step Away: Synthesize & Focus on Self-Care

Prioritizing Self-Care as a Critical Component of Effective Leadership

Leadership is a continuous and demanding journey, requiring constant decision-making, problem-solving, and the ability to support and guide others. However, effective leadership is not just about pushing forward, it also requires stepping away to recharge, reflect, and prioritize self-care. Too often, leaders overlook their own well-being, treating rest as a luxury rather than a necessity. Sustained leadership success depends on intentional self-care and mindful integration of renewal. Without prioritizing personal well-being, even the most passionate leaders risk burnout, reduced effectiveness, and emotional exhaustion. By learning to step away, leaders create space for clarity, preserve their energy, and ensure they have the resilience to lead with purpose.

This month, we will explore self-care as an essential leadership strategy rather than a personal indulgence. In Week 17, we will examine the power of pause and how intentional rest can enhance decision-making and leadership clarity. Week 18 will focus on identifying early warning signs of burnout and implementing proactive strategies for prevention. Then, in Week 19, we will shift our perspective to recognize self-care as a leadership responsibility, understanding that taking care of yourself enables you to lead more effectively and support those around you. Finally, in Week 20, we will engage in reflection and reset, using self-awareness and mindset shifts to sustain long-term leadership resilience. Stepping away is not about stepping back, it's about stepping forward with renewed energy, focus, and purpose, ensuring that you can lead effectively for the long haul.

Week 17: The Power of Pause – The Role of Rest in Leadership

Mini Lesson: Understanding how intentional breaks enhance leadership clarity.

One of the most overlooked aspects of leadership is the power of intentional rest. Early in my leadership journey, I struggled with this concept, believing that constant action was the key to success. However, over time, I realized that pausing is not a sign of weakness; it is a strategy for sustained effectiveness. Just as a cell phone battery needs to be recharged to function properly, leaders also need to step away to replenish their energy and maintain clarity. If you let your phone battery drain too low, certain functions stop working efficiently; the same happens to your body and mind when you neglect rest. Without taking time to unplug, reflect, and recharge, you risk burning out, diminished decision-making, and reduced effectiveness.

Intentional breaks are not just beneficial for you; they set an example for others, demonstrating that leadership is not about constant motion but about purposeful action. When you prioritize rest, you show your team that stepping away is a healthy and necessary part of high performance. Leadership clarity comes from moments of pause, where you can reset, refocus, and return with greater insight. To truly embrace this, be deliberate in scheduling breaks, whether it's a day off, time with family, or moments away from the office. By making rest a non-negotiable part of your leadership approach, you create the space needed for long-term success—not just for yourself, but for those you lead.

We cannot fill others when we are *empty*

Do Good LEADERSHIP

Action Step: Schedule intentional downtime in your leadership routine. This could be as simple as setting aside a few moments each day for reflection, dedicating one day a month to self-care, or planning a weekend away every few months to disconnect from work and recharge. Whether it's taking a walk, engaging in a hobby, or spending quality time with loved ones, prioritizing rest is essential for sustained leadership success. Be intentional about this time and honor it as a necessary part of your growth and effectiveness as a leader.

"Almost everything will work again if you unplug it for a few minutes... including you."

—Anne Lamott

Journal Entry: How can you integrate moments of rest into your leadership practice?

_____

_____

_____

_____

_____

_____

_____

_____

_____

_____

_____

_____

_____

_____

_____

_____

_____

_____

Week 18: Avoiding Burnout – Recognizing the Signs

> *Mini Lesson:* Identifying burnout symptoms and strategies to prevent them.

Burnout doesn't happen overnight, it builds up over time, often going unnoticed until it begins to affect your health, mindset, and performance. Recognizing the early warning signs is critical to maintaining long-term effectiveness as a leader. Are you struggling to sleep? Feeling constantly frustrated? Making poor decisions? Have you noticed yourself becoming negative with those around you? Are you experiencing unexplained health issues? Burnout can manifest in diverse ways—mentally, physically, and emotionally—causing serious challenges in both your personal and professional life. Understanding how stress impacts you personally is the first step toward addressing it before it takes a toll.

Prevention is key. Your body was not designed to sit in an office all day, remain under constant stress, or operate without breaks. Movement, fresh air, and meaningful interactions outside of work-related pressures are essential to maintaining balance. Consider taking meetings outside, incorporating walking discussions, or simply stepping away to meet a colleague for coffee with no agenda. Small, intentional shifts in how you approach your day can make a significant difference. By recognizing burnout symptoms early and integrating proactive strategies, you create a healthier, more sustainable leadership approach—one that ensures both you and your team can thrive.

Action Step: Assess your current workload and identify stress triggers. Everyone experiences stress differently and understanding what specifically overwhelms you is essential for maintaining balance. In today's fast-paced world, technology was expected to simplify tasks, yet it has often increased expectations, making workloads heavier and timelines shorter. Many leaders find themselves taking on more responsibilities with fewer resources. Take an honest look at your daily commitments, deadlines, and obligations. Identify the moments that cause the most stress and determine where adjustments can be made to create a healthier, more sustainable work-life balance.

_____

_____

_____

_____

_____

_____

"You cannot pour from an empty cup. Take care of yourself first."
—Unknown

Journal Entry: What early warning signs of burnout do you need to pay attention to?

_____

_____

_____

_____

_____

_____

_____

_____

_____

_____

_____

_____

_____

_____

_____

_____

_____

_____

Week 19: Self-Care as a Leadership Strategy

> ***Mini Lesson:*** Viewing self-care as a leadership responsibility, not a luxury.

One of the most important lessons in leadership is understanding that self-care is not a luxury—it is a responsibility. Many leaders push themselves to the limit, believing that relentless work is the key to success. However, neglecting personal well-being not only leads to burnout but also diminishes your ability to lead effectively. When you prioritize self-care, you cultivate the energy, clarity, and resilience needed to make thoughtful decisions, support your team, and navigate challenges with a steady hand. Taking care of yourself is not selfish; it is an investment in your leadership longevity and the well-being of those who rely on you.

Beyond personal benefits, modeling self-care has a powerful ripple effect within your organization. When your team sees you setting boundaries, prioritizing health, and integrating balance into your work-life approach, they are more likely to do the same. Strong leadership is not just about guiding others but also about setting an example. By demonstrating the value of self-care, you create a culture where well-being is respected, preventing burnout and fostering a healthier, more engaged team. Leadership is about sustainability, and sustainable leadership starts with a leader who recognizes that taking care of themselves is an essential part of taking care of others.

Self-care is
not a luxury

it's a
leadership necessity

Consider incorporating small self-care habits into your daily routine to maintain balance and well-being. One simple strategy is to set a timer in your office—when it goes off, step away from your screen and move. Take a walk around the building, climb a few flights of stairs, step outside to the parking lot, or, if available, use a nearby walking track. The key is to find a small, consistent action that allows you to reset and recharge.

Self-care doesn't have to be time-consuming or complicated. It could be stretching in your office, doing a quick set of wall sits, listening to a chapter of an audiobook, or even taking a moment to scroll through family photos on your phone. Find what works for you and commit to doing it daily for a week. Small, intentional acts of self-care add up over time, helping you stay energized and focused. And if all else fails, give yourself a high-five in the mirror; it's a simple but powerful reminder that you're showing up for yourself every day.

Action Step: Identify, describe, and implement a small self-care habit daily for a week.

_____

_____

_____

_____

_____

_____

_____

_____

_____

_____

_____

_____

_____

_____

_____

_____

_____

_____

"Self-care is giving the world the best of you, instead of what's left of you."
—Katie Reed

Journal Entry: What self-care practice energizes and sustains your leadership?

Self-care is essential for both your well-being and the well-being of those you lead. How can you integrate small, intentional self-care practices into your routine? Could you introduce short mindfulness moments, movement breaks, or reflection exercises in your workplace?

Sustainable leadership starts with prioritizing your energy and balance. Reflect on a self-care practice that keeps you motivated and how you can extend that habit to create a healthier, more supportive environment for those around you.

_____

_____

_____

_____

_____

_____

_____

_____

_____

_____

_____

Week 20: Reflection & Reset – Mindset Shifts for Longevity

> *Mini Lesson:* Using self-reflection as a tool for long-term leadership resilience.

Self-reflection is an essential practice for long-term leadership resilience. We often discuss the importance of pausing, but it's critical to intentionally focus on the deeper aspects of self-reflection, examining how our habits, boundaries, and priorities align with our values. Consider this in your journal entry: How does self-reflection help you synthesize and focus on self-care? As leaders, we must recognize that self-care is not an isolated task but an integrated part of a fulfilling life.

I'm reminded of how compartmentalization divides and disconnects, while integration unites and uplifts. When we treat self-care as a separate puzzle piece—distinct from family, work, and community—it can feel impossible to prioritize. However, when we embrace integration, self-care becomes more natural and sustainable. We can incorporate self-care into time with family, establish wellness habits in the workplace, or engage in self-care practices within our community. By shifting our mindset from rigid separation to seamless integration, we create a balanced approach that supports both personal well-being and leadership longevity. Self-care is not something extra—it's something essential, and when we integrate it into all areas of life, we build the resilience needed to lead effectively for the long term.

Compartmentalization Divides and Disconnects

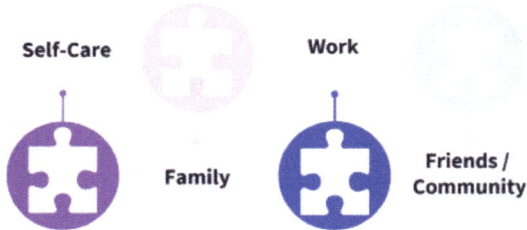

Self-Care   Work

Family   Friends / Community

Integration Unites and Uplifts

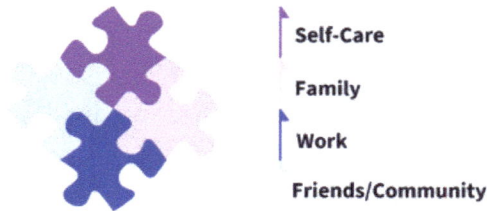

Self-Care

Family

Work

Friends/Community

Action Step: Journal about what adjustments are needed to maintain energy and focus.

_____

_____

_____

_____

_____

_____

"Rest and self-care are important. When you take time to replenish your spirit, it allows you to serve others from the overflow." —Eleanor Brownn

Journal Entry: What mindset shifts are necessary for you to sustain leadership effectiveness?

This shift requires a new mindset, as we've often been taught that balance is the key to self-care. However, balance implies a constant trade-off—like a teeter-totter, where giving more attention to one area means taking away from another. This approach can feel impossible to sustain, leading to guilt and frustration. If you focus more on self-care, you may feel like you're neglecting your family. If you prioritize work, self-care often takes a backseat.

Instead of striving for perfect balance, embrace integration as the best opportunity for success. Integration allows self-care to coexist with work, family, and community rather than competing with them. When self-care is woven into daily life, whether through shared activities with loved ones, mindful habits at work, or moments of rejuvenation within your community, it becomes a sustainable practice rather than an impossible juggling act. By shifting from balance to integration, you create a more fulfilling, resilient, and effective leadership journey.

_____

_____

_____

_____

_____

_____

STEP 6:

Step Across

Connect

Do Good
LEADERSHIP

Month 6 – Step Across:
Connect & Build Relationships

Strengthening Leadership Through Collaboration and Networking

Leadership is not a solo journey—it thrives on relationships and effective communication. This month focuses on strengthening your ability to connect with others, recognizing that leadership is as much about building trust and understanding as it is about guiding and making decisions. By stepping across, you bridge gaps, foster collaboration, and create an environment where people feel valued and heard. Strong relationships and clear communication form the foundation for a positive and effective leadership culture.

Communication crafts *connection.*

shapes *outcomes.*

and creates *culture.*

We begin with Week 21: The Power of Relationships, examining who is in your circle and how surrounding yourself with the right people impacts your leadership journey. Next, in Week 22: Communication as a Bridge, we explore how empathy, positivity, and authenticity help build trust and strengthen connections. Understanding how different people communicate is essential for success, so in Week 23: Understanding Communication Styles, we take a deeper dive into identifying various communication approaches and adapting to them for better collaboration. Finally, in Week 24: Communication Shapes Culture, we reinforce how every interaction—positive or negative—affects the overall work environment and leadership impact. Through intentional communication and strong relationships, you create a leadership style that fosters trust, connection, and long-term success.

Week 21: The Power of Relationships – Who Is in Your Circle?

__Mini Lesson:__ Recognizing the role of relationships in leadership effectiveness.

When we recognize the critical role of relationships in leadership effectiveness, everything becomes clearer. Leadership is not just about expertise, strategy, or decision-making; it is about people. Relationships are the foundation of leadership, and cultivating positive, supportive connections both inside and outside of your organization enhances your ability to lead effectively. Leadership is not meant to be a solitary path; it is strengthened through collaboration, shared experiences, and mutual growth. Strong relationships go beyond tasks and transactions; they create camaraderie, trust, and a sense of belonging that fuels both personal and professional success.

Building a network of diverse, value-driven relationships is essential because no leader is strong in every area. When you surround yourself with individuals who have different strengths, perspectives, and experiences, you create a support system that helps you navigate challenges. A well-developed network allows you to reach out for guidance, gain fresh insights, and leverage expertise where you may have gaps. The true power of relationships lies in their ability to enrich your leadership, provide new opportunities, and create a thriving, interconnected community. As you reflect on your leadership journey, ask yourself: *Who is in my circle? And how am I intentionally fostering these connections to grow and support others?*

Who's in Your Circle?

Action Step: Identify key individuals who support or challenge your leadership growth. Notice that this includes both those who encourage you and those who push you to improve. While it's natural to seek out those who affirm our efforts, true growth comes from having people in our circle who provide honest feedback, constructive criticism, and new perspectives.

To become a continually growing leader, you must embrace both encouragement and challenge as essential parts of the learning process. Surround yourself with individuals who celebrate your successes but also hold you accountable, help you recognize areas for improvement, and push you beyond your comfort zone. Growth happens when we engage with people who see our potential and challenge us to reach it, so seek out and appreciate those who help us become stronger, more effective leaders.

_____

_____

_____

_____

_____

_____

_____

_____

_____

_____

_____

_____

_____

_____

"Surround yourself with people who challenge you, teach you, and push you to be your best self."

—Bill Gates

Journal Entry: Who are the most influential people in your leadership journey? Perhaps it is a parent, perhaps it is a spouse, perhaps it is a colleague.

_____

_____

_____

_____

_____

_____

_____

_____

_____

_____

_____

_____

_____

_____

_____

_____

_____

Week 22: Communication as a Bridge – Connecting Through Empathy, Positivity, and Authenticity

> *Mini Lesson:* Strengthening leadership through meaningful communication.

Leadership is not just about speaking, it's about connecting. Effective leaders recognize that communication is the bridge that links people, ideas, and action. However, communication alone is not enough; the pillars of empathy, positivity, and authenticity must support that bridge to create meaningful, lasting relationships. Too often, leadership interactions become transactional, focused only on outcomes rather than people. But genuine connection requires seeing the individual behind the conversation, listening beyond words, and engaging with intention.

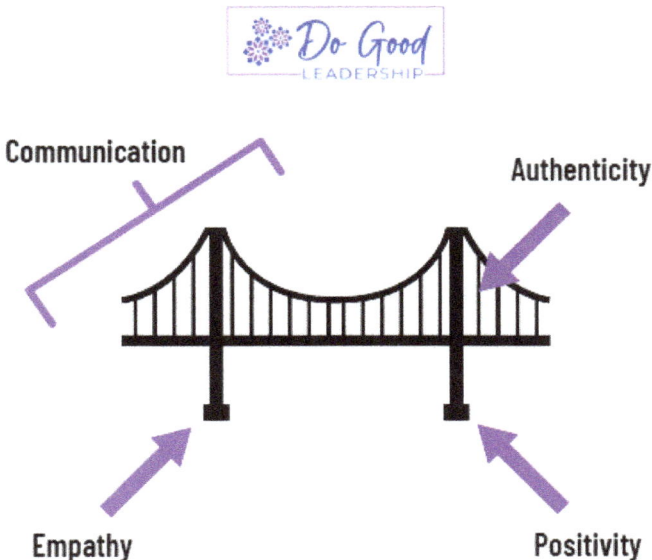

To build strong relationships, approach every interaction with curiosity and care. Ask meaningful questions—not just about work, but about the person. Do they have a family? A hobby? A unique interest? Finding common ground fosters trust and strengthens collaboration. Let's LEAD:

- Listen with empathy—pay attention to words, tone, and emotions.
- Encourage with positivity—uplift others through support and affirmation.
- Ask questions with authenticity—invite honest dialogue to deepen understanding.
- Deliver with integrity—follow through on commitments to build trust.

By integrating empathetic, positive, and authentic communication into daily leadership interactions, we create a culture where people feel valued, heard, and connected. Communication, when done with purpose, is not just a tool—it's the foundation of strong leadership and meaningful relationships.

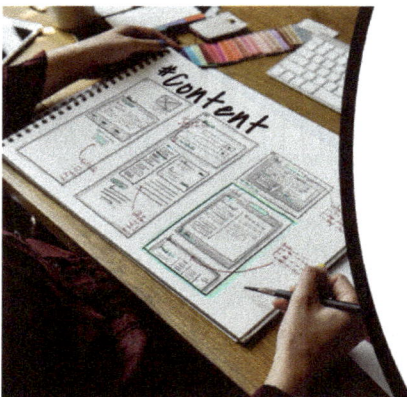

Let's LEAD

- Listen
- Encourage
- Ask Questions
- Deliver

Action Step: Engage in intentional communication today. Reach out to someone—whether a colleague, a team member, or a new connection—and focus on building a relationship, not just exchanging information. Use LEAD to listen actively, encourage openly, ask thoughtful questions, and follow through on your commitments.

_____

_____

_____

_____

_____

_____

_____

_____

_____

_____

_____

_____

_____

_____

_____

_____

_____

_____

"The art of communication is the language of leadership."

—James Humes

Journal Entry: How can you use empathetic, positive, and authentic communication to strengthen your leadership? Reflect on a recent conversation. Did you truly connect, or was it just transactional? What can you do differently moving forward?

_____

_____

_____

_____

_____

_____

_____

_____

_____

_____

_____

_____

_____

_____

_____

_____

Week 23: Understanding Communication Styles – Enhancing Connection and Success

Mini Lesson: Recognizing and adapting to different communication styles.

Effective communication is not just about delivering a message, it's about ensuring that message is understood. Too often, we assume that if we say something clearly, the recipient will interpret it exactly as we intended. However, communication is influenced by multiple factors, including personality, emotions, experiences, and individual perspectives. One of the most powerful ways to improve communication is by understanding both your own communication style and the styles of those around you. By recognizing where you and others fall on the Thinker-Feeler, Introvert-Extrovert grid, you can tailor your approach to foster stronger, more effective connections.

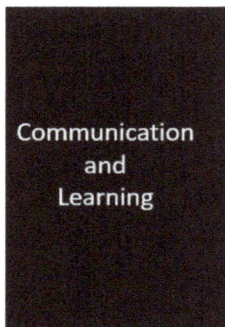

Communication and Learning

- Verbal
- Non-verbal
- Perspectives
- Experiences

The Thinker-Feeler dimension represents how individuals process and respond to information. Thinkers tend to focus on logic, facts, and data, while Feelers prioritize emotions, relationships, and empathy.

When a Thinker communicates with a Feeler, misunderstandings can arise if one person is too analytical and the other too emotionally driven. Similarly, the Introvert-Extrovert dimension affects how people engage in conversations. Extroverts are typically expressive, engaging, and thrive in group discussions, while Introverts may prefer deep, one-on-one conversations and need time to process information before responding. Understanding these differences allows leaders to adjust their communication approach—for example, giving an Introvert time to reflect before expecting a response or ensuring a Feeler feels heard before presenting logical solutions.

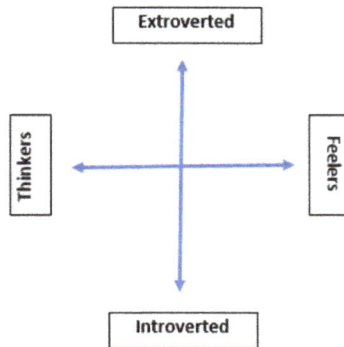

Beyond personality styles, the way we communicate is shaped by multiple factors, including verbal and non-verbal cues. The Communication Aspects Chart highlights that only 7% of communication comes from words, while 38% is conveyed through tone and 55% through body language. This means that how we say something is often more impactful than the words themselves. A leader who delivers a message with a dismissive tone or closed-off body language may unintentionally convey disinterest, even if their words are positive. Understanding these nuances is essential for building trust, fostering collaboration, and avoiding misunderstandings.

Communication Aspects

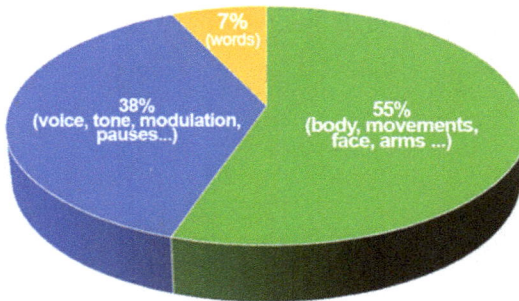

(Mehrabian, 1971)

Another critical aspect of communication is choosing the right channel. The Communication Process Model shows that encoding, decoding, and barriers impact how messages are received. While in-person communication allows for immediate clarification through tone and body language, phone conversations remove visual cues, making misunderstandings more likely. Email and text-based communication present even greater challenges, as they lack tone and non-verbal context, increasing the risk of misinterpretation. Leaders must be mindful of when and how they communicate, ensuring that complex or sensitive topics are addressed through the most effective medium.

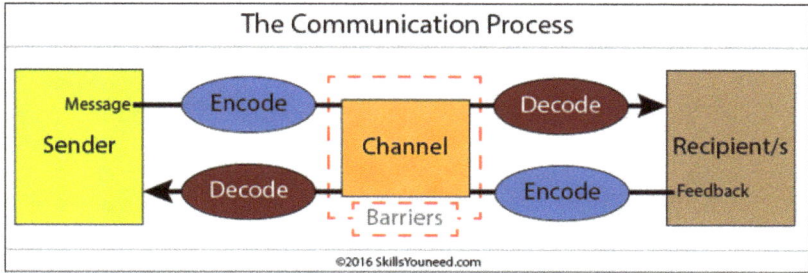

The Communication Process

Message → Sender → Encode → Channel → Decode → Recipient/s
Decode ← Barriers ← Encode ← Feedback

©2016 SkillsYouneed.com

By developing an awareness of communication styles, non-verbal cues, and the importance of message delivery, leaders can significantly improve their ability to connect, inspire, and lead effectively. Communication is not a one-size-fits-all process; rather, it requires adaptability, active listening, and a commitment to continuous improvement. When leaders take the time to understand both their own style and that of others, they strengthen relationships, reduce conflict, and create an environment where clear, impactful communication becomes the foundation of success.

Action Step: Identify your communication style on the Thinker-Feeler, Introvert-Extrovert grid. Then, observe and analyze the communication styles of those you interact with. How can you adjust your approach to improve clarity, connection, and understanding?

_____

_____

_____

_____

_____

_____

"The single biggest problem in communication is the illusion that it has taken place."

—George Bernard Shaw

Journal Entry: Reflect on a recent conversation where miscommunication may have occurred. What factors (verbal, non-verbal, tone, or perspective differences) contributed to the misunderstanding? How can you adjust your communication style to enhance clarity and connection in future interactions?

_____

_____

_____

_____

_____

_____

_____

_____

_____

_____

_____

_____

_____

_____

_____

_____

Week 24: Communication Shapes Culture – The Power of Positive and Negative Interactions

> *Mini Lesson:* How communication creates
> workplace culture.

Culture is not just one thing—it is everything. The way we communicate in the workplace defines the environment, impacts morale, and influences engagement. Communication can be seen, heard, and felt—either as a force that fosters connection, trust, and positivity, or one that breeds frustration, stress, and negativity. Research shows that negativity in the workplace leads to decreased productivity, lower commitment, and even health issues, while positive communication enhances emotional well-being, resilience, and workplace performance.

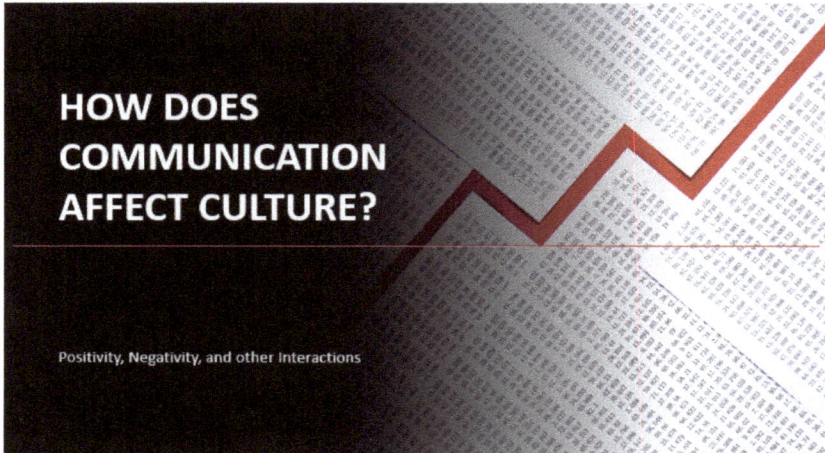

HOW DOES COMMUNICATION AFFECT CULTURE?

Positivity, Negativity, and other interactions

Consider the impact of your words, tone, and body language. When managers communicate with positivity and encouragement, employees are more likely to be engaged, motivated, and committed to their work. However, when communication is negative, dismissive, or harsh, it creates stress, disengagement, and even turnover. Studies reveal that people leave jobs not because of salary or benefits, but because of culture—and communication is at the heart of culture. Every interaction, whether in a meeting, an email, or casual conversation, contributes to the workplace atmosphere.

By being intentional about shaping communication to be clear, respectful, and constructive, leaders can create a culture that fosters collaboration, innovation, and loyalty. Positive cultures outperform negative environments, leading to better outcomes not just for individuals, but for the entire organization. As leaders, we must take responsibility for how our communication influences those around us, ensuring that we cultivate an environment where people thrive.

Action Step: Reflect on your daily communication habits. Identify one area where you can be more intentional about positive communication, whether through encouragement, tone, or active listening. Act by implementing this change today.

_____

_____

_____

_____

_____

"The culture of any organization is shaped by the worst behavior the leader is willing to tolerate."

—Gruenert & Whitaker

Journal Entry: How has workplace communication—positive or negative—impacted your job satisfaction, engagement, or performance? What steps can you take to contribute to a positive communication culture in your workplace?

_____

_____

_____

_____

_____

_____

_____

_____

_____

_____

_____

_____

_____

_____

_____

_____

The Leadership Dance

| Elevate | Step Aside: Opportunity | Step Together: Teamwork | Step Forward: Empower |

Do Good
LEADERSHIP

SECTION THREE: ELEVATE

Empowering Yourself and Others Through Leadership in Action

Leadership is not just about personal growth—it's about elevating others, creating impact, and driving meaningful change. In this final phase, Elevate, we take everything we've learned and strengthened and apply it in ways that uplift ourselves, our colleagues, and the broader community. This is where leadership transforms from an internal journey to an external force of influence and inspiration. Elevating means moving beyond personal success and stepping into a leadership role that fosters innovation, mentorship, collaboration, and advocacy for positive change in education.

Mindset Focus: Transitioning from Growth to Impact and Influence

At this stage, leadership is about vision and service—seeing beyond the immediate challenges and embracing the long-term transformation of students, peers, institutional culture, and the educational system. Visionary leaders dare to imagine new possibilities and inspire others to share in that vision. Meanwhile, service-oriented growth recognizes that true success is not just individual but collective— empowering students, supporting peers, and fostering a culture of innovation and continuous learning. Elevating means leading by example, ensuring that leadership becomes a ripple effect, positively influencing those around you.

Action: Using Leadership to Create Meaningful Change and Inspire Others

In this section, we will explore **three essential steps** to elevate leadership in action:

1. **Step Aside – Lead Through Conflict, Grow with Grace**
   Conflict is inevitable, but great leaders use it as an opportunity for connection and growth. By stepping aside from personal

biases and approaching conflict with courage, respect, and grace, leaders can reframe difficult situations, foster understanding, and build stronger relationships. Instead of viewing conflicts as barriers, we will transform them into collaborative conversations that explore differences and create solutions.

2. **Step Together – Inspire, Empower, and Lead Positively**
   Leadership is not a solo endeavor—it's about teamwork, trust, and shared growth. In this step, we embrace the ABCDs of Leadership and Learning:

   - Appreciating efforts
   - Building trust-based relationships
   - Consistency in Leadership
   - Developing and fostering growth

True leadership is about the culture and community you build—one where individuals feel valued, motivated, and empowered to succeed.

3. **Step Forward – Empower with Action**
   Leadership is about learning, preparing, and applying knowledge in motion. Using the ACTION Framework, leaders will:

   - Assess the situation
   - Clarify goals and objectives
   - Target strategies and create a plan
   - Implement the plan
   - Observe and monitor
   - Navigate adjustments

By stepping forward, leaders ensure continuous progress, innovation, and meaningful transformation in their organizations and communities.

Looking Ahead

Each of these steps—stepping aside, stepping together, and stepping forward—will be explored in depth throughout this section. Through visionary leadership, service-oriented growth, and actionable strategies, we will elevate leadership beyond personal growth and into the realm of lasting impact. True leadership isn't just about where you stand; it's about how you lift others up along the way.

The Leadership Dance
Elevate

STEP 7:
Step Aside
Opportunity

Do Good
LEADERSHIP

Month 7 – Step Aside: Transforming Challenges into Opportunities

Leading Through Conflict, Growing with Grace

Leadership is not just about moving forward, it's about knowing when to step aside, shift perspectives, and embrace challenges as opportunities for growth. Conflict, setbacks, and obstacles are inevitable, but how we approach them defines our leadership effectiveness. Strong leaders do not shy away from conflict; instead, they navigate it with courage, respect, and grace, using it to strengthen relationships, foster collaboration, and enhance problem-solving. By stepping aside from personal biases and assumptions, leaders can gain clarity, understand different perspectives, and transform difficult situations into opportunities for deeper connection and positive change.

In Week 25: Embracing Conflict as a Learning Tool, we explore how conflict can serve as a catalyst for growth when approached with openness and a willingness to listen. Week 26: Overcoming Setbacks with Resilience focuses on how to shift from a mindset of failure to one of learning, using adversity to build strength and adaptability. Providing and receiving feedback is an essential leadership skill, and in Week 27: The Art of Constructive Feedback, we examine how to communicate effectively in ways that encourage growth rather than defensiveness. Finally, in Week 28: Transforming Obstacles into Leadership Lessons, we reflect on how challenges, when reframed, can become valuable leadership opportunities. Leaders who embrace adversity with an open mind foster cultures of trust, communication, and continuous improvement, turning obstacles into stepping stones for success.

Week 25: Embracing Conflict as a Learning Tool

> *Mini Lesson:* How conflict can foster personal and professional growth.

Conflict is not something to be feared—it is an opportunity for growth, deeper understanding, and stronger collaboration. The key to leading through conflict successfully is to face it with courage, resolve it with respect, and manage it with grace. When handled well, conflict becomes a catalyst for innovation, improved relationships, and a stronger leadership presence. Instead of avoiding difficult conversations, great leaders embrace them with confidence, knowing that productive conflict can bridge gaps, enhance teamwork, and drive positive change.

At the core of graceful conflict management lies the balance of courage, respect, and grace. Courage allows us to confront difficult situations rather than avoid them. Respect ensures that we engage in open, honest conversations that honor differing perspectives. Grace enables us to manage disagreements with patience, empathy, and a commitment to finding solutions rather than placing blame. Many conflicts stem from miscommunication or unspoken expectations, but by prioritizing clear, compassionate, and solution-oriented dialogue, leaders can transform challenges into opportunities for collaboration and growth.

When leaders cultivate the ability to navigate conflict with courage, respect, and grace, they create a culture where challenges are approached with an open mind, disagreements lead to innovation, and difficult conversations strengthen rather than divide. By shifting our perspective, we turn conflict into a valuable leadership tool, using it to build trust, encourage growth, and foster meaningful connections within teams and organizations.

Lead Through Conflict. Grow With Grace

Action Step: Identify a past conflict and outline how it led to growth. For instance, if you had a conflicted issue, how did that help you? How did you shift your perspective and grow to learn and develop moving forward?

_____

_____

_____

"In the middle of difficulty
lies opportunity."
—Albert Einstein

Journal Entry: How can you shift your mindset to see conflict as a growth opportunity?

_____

_____

_____

_____

_____

_____

_____

_____

_____

_____

_____

_____

_____

_____

_____

_____

_____

Week 26: Overcoming Setbacks with Resilience

> ***Mini Lesson:*** Building resilience by learning from failures.

Setbacks are not roadblocks; they are opportunities for growth, self-awareness, and leadership refinement. Too often, when faced with failure, we react with frustration, disappointment, or self-doubt, believing that things are falling apart. However, setbacks provide some of the most valuable lessons in leadership—they challenge us to adapt, strengthen our decision-making, and develop the resilience needed to navigate future obstacles. The key is to shift our perspective: instead of seeing setbacks as failures, we must recognize them as opportunities to reflect, refine our approach, and emerge stronger.

One of the most effective ways to transform setbacks into opportunities is through self-reflection. Keeping a journal of your leadership journey—documenting decisions, challenges, and lessons learned—allows you to track your progress and turn past struggles into a foundation for future success. When we take time to reflect, we realize that even the most difficult situations have taught us something valuable—whether it's improving communication, learning to navigate conflict, or developing patience and adaptability. These experiences help us lead with greater wisdom and empathy.

Setbacks also provide opportunities to pivot and innovate. Some of the greatest breakthroughs in leadership and business come from moments of failure that force people to rethink their strategies. When things do not go as planned, it opens the door for innovative ideas, fresh perspectives, and creative problem-solving. A leader who views setbacks as opportunities to reassess, adjust, and grow will ultimately be more effective, adaptable, and confident in guiding others through change.

Resilience is not about avoiding difficulties but about facing them head-on, learning from them, and using those lessons to bridge gaps, build stronger relationships, and lead with authenticity. Every challenge you have overcome has prepared you for the next opportunity. As you navigate future obstacles, remember that setbacks are not signs of weakness but evidence of growth in motion. By reflecting, learning, and applying new insights, you are continuously strengthening your foundation, ensuring that each challenge makes you a more adaptable, empathetic, and effective leader.

Action Step: List three past setbacks and what you learned from them. Really be clear and detailed here.

_____

_____

_____

_____

_____

_____

_____

_____

_____

_____

_____

_____

_____

_____

_____

_____

_____

_____

"Our greatest glory is not in never falling,
but in rising every time we fall."
—Confucius

Journal Entry: How has a past failure shaped your leadership?

_____

_____

_____

_____

_____

_____

_____

_____

_____

_____

_____

_____

_____

_____

_____

_____

_____

_____

_____

Week 27: The Art of Constructive Feedback

Mini Lesson: Giving and receiving feedback with impact.

Feedback is one of the most valuable tools for personal and professional growth, but many people resist it due to fear of criticism or judgment. Constructive feedback is not about pointing out flaws—it's about providing insights that help individuals improve, refine their skills, and strengthen relationships. There are two key types of feedback: internal and external. Internal feedback comes from self-reflection, where we assess our own actions, decisions, and areas for improvement. External feedback comes from colleagues, mentors, or team members, offering perspectives that we may not see ourselves. However, feedback is only useful when we are open to receiving it with a mindset of learning rather than defensiveness.

Constructive Feedback

The Emotional
Intelligence Factor

Feedback with
positive impact

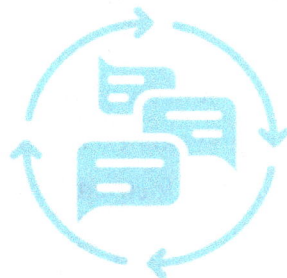

Do Good
LEADERSHIP

The Role of Emotional Intelligence (EI) in Communication

Emotional intelligence plays a critical role in how we give and receive feedback, shaping our ability to communicate effectively and with intention. Self-awareness allows us to recognize our emotions and communicate authentically without letting defensiveness cloud our judgment. Empathy helps us understand the emotions and perspectives of others, making feedback conversations more productive and constructive. Self-regulation ensures we manage emotional reactions, preventing impulsive responses that could shut down growth opportunities. Social skills, such as active listening and clear expression, build trust and rapport, ensuring that feedback is delivered and received in a way that encourages mutual respect and learning.

The Role of Emotional Intelligence in Conflict Resolution

Feedback, especially when critical, can sometimes lead to conflict or emotional discomfort. This is where emotional intelligence helps navigate difficult conversations with grace and effectiveness. Facilitating understanding through empathy allows us to see feedback as an opportunity rather than an attack, improving collaboration and team dynamics. Managing emotions through self-regulation prevents escalation, ensuring that feedback discussions remain solution-focused rather than emotionally charged. Effective communication skills, such as active listening and clearly expressing concerns, ensure that both the giver and receiver of feedback engage in productive dialogue rather than defensiveness. High EI also builds trust, making it easier for individuals to accept and implement feedback without resentment. Lastly, motivation for resolution encourages individuals to embrace feedback as a tool for growth, seeing it as a pathway to improvement rather than a personal critique.

Applying Constructive Feedback with Impact

The best leaders embrace feedback as a gift, using it to strengthen their leadership skills, improve communication, and foster growth in those around them. When delivering feedback, ensure it is clear, constructive, and focused on development rather than criticism. When receiving feedback, listen with an open mind, reflect before responding, and apply what is useful to enhance your leadership effectiveness. By integrating emotional intelligence into feedback and conflict resolution, you create an environment where feedback is welcomed, valued, and seen as a pathway to continuous learning and success.

Action Step: Practice delivering constructive feedback to a colleague or team member.

_____

_____

_____

_____

_____

_____

"Feedback is the breakfast of champions." —Ken Blanchard

Journal Entry: Reflect on the time you received constructive feedback. How did it help you grow?

_____

_____

_____

_____

_____

_____

_____

_____

_____

_____

_____

_____

_____

_____

_____

As you receive feedback, use it as a learning opportunity to refine how you provide constructive feedback to others. Effective feedback is not just about pointing out what went wrong or what could have been done differently, it is about offering insights that encourage growth and improvement. Instead of simply stating what was ineffective, consider framing your feedback with thought-provoking questions: "Have you considered this approach? Did you notice the impact this had on others?" This method invites reflection rather than defensiveness, making the feedback more impactful.

Constructive feedback should provide both guidance and opportunities for improvement. It should offer clear, specific insights while encouraging the recipient to explore alternative perspectives and strategies. By focusing on growth rather than criticism, you create a supportive environment where feedback is seen as a tool for learning and positive change, fostering both development and adaptability.

Week 28: Transforming Obstacles Into Leadership Lessons

> ***Mini Lesson:*** Shifting perspective to see challenges as stepping stones.

Leadership is not about avoiding obstacles—it's about learning how to navigate them with purpose, strategy, and resilience. Too often, we see challenges as burdens, roadblocks, or weights holding us back, rather than opportunities to grow, innovate, and strengthen our leadership abilities. But what if we could shift our perspective? What if, instead of viewing obstacles as problems, we saw them as stepping stones to success?

Shifting your focus transforms *Obstacles* into *Opportunities*

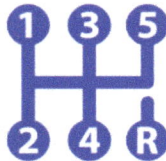

Think of leadership like driving a manual transmission car. Manual leaders don't just cruise; they engage. They are actively shifting gears, adjusting to the terrain, and making strategic choices in real-time. When the road gets tough, they downshift to gain control, and when momentum builds, they kick into high gear to accelerate progress. Unlike an automatic car, where the vehicle makes the decisions for you, a manual transmission leader is intentional, adaptable, and fully present. One wrong shift and you stall in front of the whole team—that's accountability! But when you embrace the challenge, you learn to manage each turn, each incline, and each detour with confidence. The best leaders don't just react; they shift with intention.

So, when you face a challenge, do not stare at the peak of the mountain, and feel overwhelmed. Instead, focus on the next step in front of you. Break it down into manageable actions—one shift, one adjustment at a time. Every challenge presents a chance to refine your skills, assess your resilience, and strengthen your leadership. Just as a skilled driver learns to anticipate the road ahead, great leaders develop the ability to see challenges not as obstacles, but as opportunities for growth and transformation. Do you want to be an automatic leader, letting circumstances dictate your journey, or a manual leader, fully engaged in every turn and decision?

Step Up and SHIFT

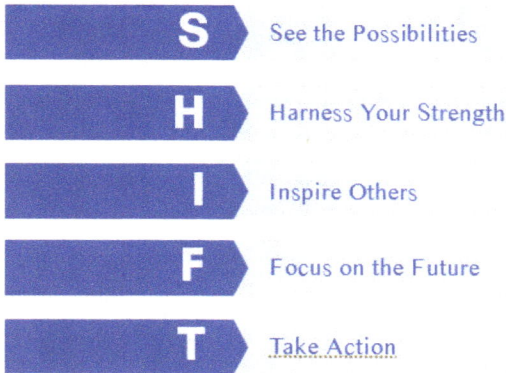

S — See the Possibilities

H — Harness Your Strength

I — Inspire Others

F — Focus on the Future

T — Take Action

Do Good LEADERSHIP

Step Up and SHIFT

S.H.I.F.T. stands for:

- S – See the possibilities – Open your mind to new opportunities and envision the growth that change can bring.
- H – Harness your strengths – Use your unique skills and talents to navigate through transformation with confidence.
- I – Inspire others – Lead by example, motivating those around you to embrace the shift and adapt with grace.
- F – Focus on the future – Keep your eye on the bigger picture, driving change with a clear sense of direction and purpose.
- T – Take action – Move forward with intention, making decisions and taking steps that drive transformation and growth.

By embracing this mindset, you don't just overcome obstacles, you turn them into opportunities that shape you into a stronger, more impactful leader.

Action Step: Identify a recent challenge and list potential leadership lessons from it.

_____

_____

_____

_____

_____

_____

_____

_____

_____

_____

_____

_____

_____

_____

"Difficulties strengthen the mind, as labor does the body."

—Seneca

Journal Entry: How can you approach challenges differently in the future?

_____

_____

_____

_____

_____

_____

_____

_____

_____

_____

_____

_____

_____

_____

_____

_____

_____

The Leadership Dance
Elevate

STEP 8:
Step Together
Teamwork

Do Good
LEADERSHIP

Month 8 – Step Together: Building a Collaborative Leadership Culture

Leadership is not about standing alone at the top; it is about uniting people, fostering trust, and creating a culture where everyone contributes and thrives. True leadership is strengthened through collaboration, innovation, and shared success. When individuals feel valued, included, and empowered, they become invested in the team's mission, working with greater dedication and purpose. Stepping together means shifting from an individual mindset to a collective movement, where leadership is not about authority but about inspiring, supporting, and elevating others.

In Week 29: The Power of Teamwork, we explore how strong leaders cultivate synergy, leveraging diverse strengths to achieve common goals. Week 30: Creating an Inclusive Leadership Environment emphasizes the importance of ensuring that every voice is heard and valued, making inclusion a driving force for team success. Trust becomes the foundation of effective leadership in Week 31: Trust & Accountability in Teams, highlighting how mutual respect and responsibility strengthen relationships and build confidence. Finally, in Week 32: Leadership as Service – Giving Back, we shift the focus from individual achievements to leadership as a means of service, reinforcing that true impact comes from lifting others and contributing to the greater good.

By fostering a culture built on collaboration, trust, and shared leadership, leaders create environments where people feel empowered to contribute and grow. Stepping together is about cultivating teams that are strong, engaged, and committed to a shared vision—where leadership is not just about achieving results, but about making a lasting, meaningful impact.

Week 29: The Power of Teamwork

Mini Lesson: Why collaboration strengthens leadership.

Building a collaborative leadership culture is essential because culture is everything. As leadership expert Jon Gordon emphasizes, a strong culture determines the success of a team, organization, or movement. In this lesson, we focus on the power of teamwork and how collaboration strengthens leadership. We've all heard the saying, "There is no 'I' in team," but effective teamwork goes beyond just working together—it requires intentional communication, shared vision, and trust. Creating a high-performing team means understanding the diverse strengths, experiences, and perspectives that each member brings. No single leader has all the answers, and true leadership is recognizing the value of collective intelligence. By fostering collaboration, leaders enhance creativity, problem-solving, and productivity, ensuring that everyone has a role in driving success.

However, teamwork doesn't happen by chance; it must be built with purpose. Strong teams are rooted in trust, aligned in vision, and committed to supporting one another. This means laying the foundation for effective communication, embracing different personalities, and ensuring that all voices are heard. When collaboration is done well, it inspires, empowers, and leads positively, creating an environment where individuals thrive, innovation flourishes, and leadership is shared. As you reflect on your role within a team, consider how you can contribute to a culture of collaboration, uplift those around you, and leverage the collective strengths of your team to achieve greater success than any one person could accomplish alone.

Teamwork:
Inspire.
Empower.
and lead
Positively

Action Step: Identify one way you can improve teamwork in your environment.

_____

_____

_____

_____

_____

_____

_____

_____

_____

"Alone we can do little;
together we can do much."
—Helen Keller

Journal Entry: Describe a time when collaboration led to success.

_____

_____

_____

_____

_____

_____

_____

_____

_____

_____

_____

_____

_____

_____

_____

_____

_____

_____

Week 30: Creating an Inclusive Leadership Environment

> *Mini Lesson:* The value of inclusion in leadership and teamwork.

Inclusion in leadership is about ensuring that diverse perspectives, experiences, and voices are truly valued and integrated into decision-making. Too often, teams are created with a predetermined outcome in mind, where leaders assemble individuals they believe will align with their vision rather than challenge it. While this may seem efficient, it eliminates true collaboration and limits innovation. A strong and effective team is not one that always agrees but one that engages in meaningful discussion, considers multiple viewpoints, and strengthens ideas through diverse contributions. Leaders must welcome differing opinions, even when they slow the process, because those voices help identify gaps, refine strategies, and create well-rounded, inclusive solutions.

An inclusive leadership environment is built on trust, appreciation, and consistency—principles reflected in the ABCD of Leadership: Appreciation, Building Relationships, Consistency, and Development. Leaders must appreciate all contributions, not just those that align with their own thinking. Building relationships based on trust and openness encourages individuals to speak up without fear of dismissal. Consistency in valuing all voices fosters an environment where collaboration thrives, and development ensures that every team member has the opportunity to grow and contribute meaningfully. Inclusion is not about checking a box—it is about intentionally creating a culture where everyone's voice matters. By embracing diversity of thought and fostering a space for open dialogue, leaders strengthen teams, enhance decision-making, and build a leadership culture rooted in equity and growth.

The ABCD
of Leadership

A Appreciation

Building Relationships

C Consistency

Development

Action Step: Take time this week to assess how inclusive your leadership approach is by gathering feedback from diverse team members, reflecting on your practices, and identifying at least one specific adjustment you can implement to foster a more inclusive environment.

_____

_____

_____

_____

_____

_____

"Diversity is being invited to the party; inclusion is being asked to dance."
—Verna Myers

Journal Entry: How can you ensure all voices are heard in your leadership?

_____

_____

_____

_____

_____

_____

_____

_____

_____

_____

_____

_____

_____

_____

_____

_____

_____

Week 31: Trust & Accountability in Teams

> ***Mini Lesson:*** Building trust as a leadership foundation.

Trust is the cornerstone of effective leadership and teamwork. It is not built overnight, nor is it granted by default—it must be earned through consistent actions, honesty, and reliability. Unlike a simple handshake, true trust is developed over time through transparency, follow-through, and mutual respect. When team members know they can count on one another, they collaborate more effectively, communicate openly, and feel a sense of security in their roles. However, trust is fragile—it takes time to build, but only a moment to break. Factors that strengthen trust include honesty, consistency, accountability, and follow-through—when leaders and team members do what they say they will do, trust deepens. Conversely, trust is broken when individuals fail to meet commitments, lack transparency, or demonstrate dishonesty. A team without trust is simply a group of people working together, but a team with trust is a force that moves forward with shared purpose and unity.

Alongside trust, accountability is essential for ensuring success. Without accountability, trust cannot be sustained. For teams to function effectively, clear expectations, defined roles, and shared goals must be established from the start. Each team member should understand their responsibilities and feel a sense of ownership over their contributions. Accountability is not about blame or micromanagement—it is about taking responsibility for one's role while ensuring the team moves forward together. Leaders must create a culture where trust and accountability go hand in hand by giving team members the TIME they need to build relationships, reinforce commitments, and maintain integrity. A team that trusts one another and holds each other accountable is one that will withstand challenges, grow stronger through adversity, and achieve lasting success.

Action Step: Implement one strategy to improve trust in your team.

_____

_____

_____

_____

_____

_____

_____

_____

"Trust is the glue of life.
It is the foundational principle that holds
all relationships."
—Stephen Covey

Journal Entry: What trust-building actions can you take as a leader?

_____

_____

_____

_____

_____

_____

_____

_____

_____

_____

_____

_____

_____

_____

_____

_____

_____

Week 32: Leadership as Service – Giving Back

> ***Mini Lesson:*** The importance of servant leadership.

Leadership is not about titles, power, or accolades—it is about service, impact, and elevating those around you. A true leader understands that their role is not to stand alone at the top but to empower others to rise with them. At the heart of servant leadership is the shift from self-serving to selfless leadership—leading not for personal gain but for the betterment of the team, the organization, and the community. If leadership is solely about personal success, recognition, and control, then it becomes hollow and unsustainable. While awards and achievements may provide temporary validation, true leadership legacy is built on how many others you uplift along the way. Servant leaders create a culture of support, collaboration, and purpose, ensuring that everyone feels valued, heard, and empowered.

However, servant leadership does not mean giving yourself to the point of exhaustion or sacrificing your well-being. It is about choosing, every day, to lead with care, integrity, and accountability. It is about being willing to do the trivial things that contribute to a greater purpose, for example, picking up a piece of trash on campus instead of assuming it's someone else's responsibility. Servant leadership is about modeling the behaviors you want to see in your team and showing that no task is beneath you. When you lead with service, you inspire a culture where people take ownership, support one another, and work toward a shared vision. Leadership is not about commanding, it is about choosing daily to be the type of leader who serves, elevates, and makes a meaningful difference.

"COMING TOGETHER IS BEGINNING

KEEPING TOGETHER IS PROGRESS

WORKING TOGETHER IS SUCCESS."

Henry Ford

Action Step: Find one way to give back as a leader this week.

_____

_____

_____

_____

_____

_____

_____

_____

_____

_____

"The best way to find yourself is to lose yourself in the service of others."
—Mahatma Gandhi

Journal Entry: How has serving others influenced your leadership?

_____

_____

_____

_____

_____

_____

_____

_____

_____

_____

_____

_____

_____

_____

_____

_____

_____

STEP 9:

Step Forward

Empower

Do Good
LEADERSHIP

Month 9 – Step Forward:
Action-Driven Leadership

Leadership is not about standing still, it is about taking action, making decisions, and moving forward with confidence. The most effective leaders step forward with courage, take initiative, and embrace the responsibility of driving meaningful change. Week 33: The Courage to Take Initiative highlights the importance of proactive leadership, encouraging leaders to step up rather than wait for permission. Leadership also requires Week 34: Implementing Bold Leadership Moves, where taking calculated risks fosters innovation, pushes boundaries, and propels teams toward success. True leadership is not about avoiding challenges but about embracing them with confidence and adaptability.

Learn, prepare and practice in *motion.*

apply, achieve, and advance with *action*

However, leadership does not stop with personal achievement, it extends to developing and empowering the next generation. In Week 35: Developing Future Leaders, we explore the responsibility of mentoring, guiding, and equipping others with the tools to lead effectively. Finally, Week 36: Measuring Impact and Growth focuses on reflection, evaluation, and refining leadership strategies to ensure lasting progress. Success in leadership is not about achieving perfection but about maintaining momentum, learning from experience, and continually striving for meaningful impact.

This month challenges you to take bold action, apply what you've learned, and step forward with purpose. Leadership is not just about having great ideas, it is about executing them with confidence, driving real change, and inspiring others to do the same.

Week 33: The Courage to Take Initiative

> ***Mini Lesson:*** Recognizing the power of proactive leadership.

Proactive leadership is about stepping forward, anticipating challenges, and taking action before problems arise. It requires foresight, adaptability, and the willingness to make decisions that shape the future. Effective leaders do not simply react to situations—they prepare for them, learn from past experiences, and use reflection to guide their next steps. One of the most powerful ways to strengthen proactive leadership is through intentional reflection, whether through journaling, mentorship discussions, or analyzing past decisions to recognize patterns and opportunities for growth. The more you reflect on experiences, the more you develop the ability to anticipate and address challenges with confidence.

Taking initiative also means staying engaged, connected, and attuned to the environment around you. This could be as simple as walking through your office or organization, checking in with your team, and understanding their needs before they escalate into challenges. It could involve sharing insights, offering support, or providing guidance before a major decision is made. The most effective leaders do not wait for opportunities to come to them; they create them. Leadership is about being present, understanding the culture, and knowing what works best for your team. By stepping forward with courage, you empower yourself and those around you to grow, innovate, and lead with confidence.

Action Step: Identify one area where you've previously hesitated to take initiative—whether it's speaking up in meetings, leading a project, or proposing a new idea—and take one concrete action this week to move forward with confidence.

_____

_____

_____

_____

_____

_____

_____

_____

_____

_____

_____

_____

_____

_____

_____

_____

_____

_____

"The way to get started is to quit talking and begin doing."
—Walt Disney

Journal Entry: What is one bold leadership move you have been avoiding? Why?

_____

_____

_____

_____

_____

_____

_____

_____

_____

_____

_____

_____

_____

_____

_____

_____

Week 34: Implementing Bold Leadership Moves

> *Mini Lesson:* Taking calculated risks in leadership.

Leadership is not about playing it safe, it is about recognizing when to take bold, calculated risks that drive meaningful change. Throughout history, leadership has followed a pendulum effect, shifting between stability and transformation. Sometimes, change comes from the top down, driven by institutional leaders such as presidents, chancellors, or governing bodies. At other times, shifts emerge from the ground up, initiated by faculty, students, or even the broader community. External factors, such as economic shifts, policy changes, or global events like the pandemic, have also forced leaders to adapt rapidly and make high-stakes decisions. In these moments, leaders must embrace uncertainty, gather critical information, and determine the best course of action. Great leaders are not defined by avoiding risk but by their ability to take strategic, well-informed risks that lead to progress.

Taking bold leadership moves requires a balance of courage, preparation, and adaptability. Leaders must assess situations carefully, consult with trusted advisors, and collaborate with a team to evaluate the potential impact of their decisions. Whether working with a formal leadership team, a small advisory group, or external mentors, leveraging collective wisdom can help clarify potential risks and rewards. Not every bold move will succeed, but true leadership means having the resilience to take ownership of decisions, learn from outcomes, and adjust accordingly. Leadership is about action, not hesitation. By stepping forward with intention and embracing the ACTION framework—Assess, Clarify, Target, Implement, Observe, and Navigate—leaders can make informed, bold choices that shape the future of their teams and organizations.

Take **ACTION**

Do Good
LEADERSHIP

A — Assess the Situation

C — Clarify Goals/Objectives

T — Target Strategies/Plan

I — Implement the Plan

O — Observe and Monitor

N — Navigate Adjustments

Action Step: Choose one bold action that aligns with your goals—such as starting a new project, initiating a difficult conversation, or applying for a leadership opportunity—and outline three specific steps you will take this week to begin executing it with intention.

_____

_____

_____

_____

_____

"Fortune favors the bold."
—Virgil

Journal Entry: What bold action did you commit to this week, and what steps did you take to begin executing it? Reflect on how it challenged you, what you learned in the process, and how it moved you closer to your leadership goals?

_____

_____

_____

_____

_____

_____

_____

_____

_____

_____

_____

_____

_____

_____

_____

_____

_____

_____

_____

Week 35: Developing Future Leaders

> ***Mini Lesson:*** The responsibility of mentoring and developing others.

Leadership is not about climbing to the top alone; it is about lifting others as you rise. Unfortunately, many aspiring leaders, particularly women, have experienced the harsh reality of being stepped on or pushed aside by others seeking power or advancement. Too often, leadership becomes a competition rather than a collaborative effort to build a stronger, more inclusive future. But true leadership means creating opportunities for others, not closing doors behind you. As a leader, your responsibility is to embrace the role of mentorship, empower others with guidance and support, and encourage those who are eager to grow. This is not just about filling positions; it is about shaping the future of leadership by investing in people who are eager to learn, develop, and make a difference.

Look for those with enthusiasm, curiosity, and a willingness to grow. Future leaders are not always the loudest voices in the room, they are often the ones who ask thoughtful questions, seek guidance, and show a hunger for learning. Mentorship does not have to be a formal program. It can be as simple as offering advice, sharing experiences, or providing encouragement when someone needs it most. If you have had a mentor, you understand the profound impact that guidance can have. And if you have never had one, then be the mentor you wish you had. Embrace your role in developing others, empower them with the knowledge and confidence to step into leadership, and embrace the responsibility of fostering a culture of support, growth, and shared success. Leadership is not about accumulating power; it is about creating a legacy by developing and empowering those who will lead after you.

Empowered Women Empower Women

EMBRAVE.
EMBRACE.
EMPOWER.

Do Good
LEADERSHIP

Action Step: Identify someone to mentor and create a plan to support their growth. Start small—perhaps with one person—and allow the relationship to develop naturally. Over time, you may find yourself mentoring a group or even creating a formal program to develop future leaders.

_____

_____

_____

_____

_____

_____

"Empower others and you empower yourself."
—Unknown

Journal Entry: How have mentors shaped your leadership journey?

_____

_____

_____

_____

_____

_____

_____

_____

_____

_____

_____

_____

_____

_____

_____

_____

_____

Week 36: Measuring Impact and Growth

> ***Mini Lesson:*** Evaluating leadership progress and areas for improvement.

Leadership is a continuous journey of growth, reflection, and refinement. The key to becoming a better leader is not just about taking action but also about assessing the impact of those actions. Effective leaders regularly evaluate their progress, identify areas for improvement, and adjust their approach to better serve their teams and organizations. Ask yourself: *Am I where I want to be as a leader? Am I fostering a positive, supportive culture? Am I leading authentically and consistently?* These are not just questions to reflect on privately—true growth requires seeking honest feedback from colleagues, mentors, and those you lead. It is easy to assume you are doing well, but real leadership growth happens when you embrace constructive feedback, both positive and negative, and use it as a tool for improvement.

Measuring Impact and Growth

Evaluation goes beyond personal reflection—it is about aligning your leadership with your long-term goals. Are you effective in communication, collaboration, and decision-making? Do you need to develop new skills or strengthen existing ones? Maybe you are considering a new leadership direction, such as moving from academics to student services, technical careers, or workforce development. The path you take should be intentional, driven by a clear understanding of your strengths and areas for growth. Leadership is not about reaching a final destination—it is about constant learning, adapting, and improving. By measuring your progress and seeking growth opportunities, you ensure that your leadership continues to evolve, inspire, and create lasting impact.

Action Step: Assess your leadership effectiveness through feedback or reflection.

_____

_____

_____

_____

_____

_____

_____

_____

_____

_____

_____

_____

_____

_____

_____

_____

_____

"What gets measured gets improved."
—Peter Drucker

Journal Entry: How do you measure your leadership growth?

_____

_____

_____

_____

_____

_____

_____

_____

_____

_____

_____

_____

_____

_____

_____

_____

_____

_____

_____

_____

_____

The Leadership Dance

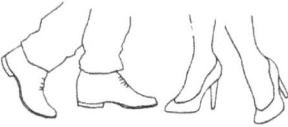

Reflect & Renew

Do Good
LEADERSHIP

SECTION FOUR: REFLECT & RENEW

Sustaining Your Leadership Through Purposeful Pause and Strategic Planning

Leadership is a journey, not a destination—and every journey requires moments of stillness, clarity, and renewal. In this final stage, Reflect & Renew, we bring our 36 week leadership transformation full circle. After months of stepping up, stepping in, stepping out, and elevating others, this section invites us to pause with intention— to look back with gratitude, take inventory of our growth, and re-center ourselves for the path ahead.

True leadership is sustained not just by vision or energy but by reflection and strategic renewal. Without space to breathe, leaders burn out. Without recalibration, even the most passionate leaders can lose direction. Reflect & Renew is about preserving your purpose, staying grounded in your "why," and building systems that help your leadership not only last—but evolve.

This is not a passive phase. In fact, it's one of the most powerful. Because it's here—in the stillness—that leaders find the clarity to go further, the courage to let go of what no longer serves them, and the wisdom to lead from a place of deep authenticity. Reflection cultivates resilience. Renewal restores resolve. Together, they empower you to continue leading with strength, vision, and impact long after this journey ends.

Mindset Focus: Sustaining Impact Through Clarity, Renewal, and Purpose-Driven Leadership

At this stage, leadership is about intentional sustainability. You've done the deep inner work. You've taken action and inspired others. Now it's time to ensure that the progress you've made is protected, maintained, and elevated into the future.

Reflective leaders don't react—they respond with awareness and intention. They pause to assess what's working, release what's not, and re-align with what truly matters. Renewal isn't about starting over—it's about re-engaging with purpose, refining your focus, and embracing seasons of growth and rest as equally vital.

A leader committed to longevity understands that clarity fuels momentum, and reflection ensures that every step forward is anchored in meaning. As you move through this phase, allow yourself to be both proud of how far you've come and honest about what needs to evolve next.

Action Focus: Develop a Sustainable Leadership Plan That Reflects, Refines, and Renews Your Impact

This final section challenges you to integrate all the insights, strategies, and skills you've developed into a sustainable leadership roadmap. Through structured reflection, celebration, intentional self-care, and future-focused planning, you'll walk away with a vision and plan that keeps your leadership aligned, impactful, and energized—long-term.

What's Ahead in the Final Three Months?

In the final three months of your leadership journey, the focus shifts toward sustainability, reflection, and future impact. In Month 10, the emphasis is on self-care for sustained leadership. True leadership longevity requires intentional practices that prioritize well-being— not as an afterthought, but as a cornerstone of success. You'll explore how to recognize and prevent leadership fatigue, understand the role of gratitude in fulfillment, maintain long-term growth, and harness emotional intelligence to support endurance and effectiveness. In Month 11, you'll turn inward to reflect, celebrate, and strategize. This is a time to acknowledge your leadership milestones, celebrate your progress, and honor the people who've supported your growth. You'll use those insights to evaluate and refine your leadership style and begin shaping a long-term strategy. Then, in Month 12, your attention turns forward with vision and goal setting for continued, impactful leadership. Leadership doesn't end—it evolves. You'll craft a personal leadership vision statement, align your daily actions with your long-term purpose, and create a concrete plan for year-round growth. You'll also define the leadership legacy you want to leave, ensuring your impact endures well beyond this season.

A Leadership Journey That Never Ends

This section is not an ending but a transition—a bridge between where you've been and where you're going next. Leadership is a continuous process of learning, growing, and refining. The Reflect & Renew phase ensures that your leadership journey does not stop here but instead becomes a cycle of sustained impact and continuous evolution.

Are you ready to take all that you've learned and use it to create lasting leadership success? Let's step forward with confidence, clarity, and purpose.

Month 10 – Self-Care for Sustained Leadership

Leadership is a long-term commitment, and without intentional self-care, even the most passionate and dedicated leaders can experience fatigue, burnout, or emotional exhaustion. Sustained leadership requires balance, resilience, and a mindset that prioritizes well-being. This month, we focus on strategies to prevent leadership fatigue, recognizing the signs of burnout before they take a toll on your health and effectiveness. Reflection and gratitude are essential in this process, allowing leaders to pause, appreciate their journey, and acknowledge the people and moments that have contributed to their growth. By practicing gratitude and reflection, you create a leadership culture that fosters motivation, connection, and long-term fulfillment.

True leadership longevity is about more than just avoiding burnout, it is about continuing to grow, evolve, and sustain impact over time. Developing strong emotional intelligence is a crucial part of this, as it allows leaders to navigate stress, foster meaningful relationships, and communicate with clarity and empathy. This month, you will explore the role of emotional intelligence in leadership sustainability, as well as strategies for long-term leadership success. The key to sustained leadership is not just working harder, but working smarter—integrating self-care, reflection, and emotional awareness into your daily leadership practice. When you take care of yourself, you can lead with greater energy, clarity, and purpose, ensuring that your leadership remains strong, impactful, and fulfilling.

Week 37 focuses on preventing leadership fatigue, helping you recognize the warning signs of burnout and prioritize intentional self-care as an essential part of your leadership practice. You'll explore strategies to support your physical, emotional, and mental well-being so you can sustain your leadership over the long term. Week 38 highlights reflection and gratitude in leadership, showing how practicing gratitude can strengthen both your leadership fulfillment and your team's motivation. You'll learn that small, meaningful moments of acknowledgment and appreciation can have a powerful ripple effect on those around you. Week 39 centers on leadership longevity strategies, encouraging you to view leadership as a lifelong journey of learning and growth. You'll identify habits and practices that support your continued development, helping you stay engaged, relevant, and impactful as a leader over time. Week 40 emphasizes the importance of emotional intelligence, guiding you to improve self-awareness, empathy, and communication in your leadership approach. You'll discover how developing emotional intelligence helps you navigate challenges, build stronger relationships, and lead with greater effectiveness and resilience.

Week 37: Preventing Leadership Fatigue

> ***Mini Lesson:*** Recognizing the signs of burnout and taking preventive measures.

Burnout is a real and serious challenge for leaders. Many professionals in education and leadership experience chronic stress, emotional exhaustion, and mental fatigue. Burnout is not something that happens overnight, it accumulates over time and, if ignored, can lead to disengagement, dissatisfaction, and even departure from leadership roles.

Leadership Fatigue

To prevent burnout, you must recognize its warning signs. These can include feeling constantly overwhelmed, struggling with decision fatigue, losing motivation, experiencing physical symptoms like headaches or sleep disturbances, and feeling emotionally drained. Sustainable leadership requires intentional self-care—not as an afterthought, but as an essential part of your daily routine.

Action Step: Identify self-care habits that support longevity in leadership. Consider hydration, movement, healthy eating, mindfulness, and setting boundaries for work-life integration.

_____

_____

_____

_____

_____

_____

_____

_____

_____

_____

_____

_____

_____

_____

_____

_____

"If you don't take the time to rest, your body will take the time for you."
—Unknown

Journal Entry: How can you integrate self-care into your leadership routine? Reflect on ways to build sustainable wellness habits into your daily leadership approach.

_____

_____

_____

_____

_____

_____

_____

_____

_____

_____

_____

_____

_____

_____

_____

_____

_____

Week 38: Reflection & Gratitude in Leadership

> *Mini Lesson:* The role of gratitude in leadership fulfillment.

Gratitude is a transformational leadership tool. It is not just about saying "thank you"—it is about acknowledging, appreciating, and recognizing the people and moments that contribute to success. Leaders who cultivate gratitude not only create a more positive and motivated team environment but also increase their own fulfillment and resilience.

Reflection & Gratitude in Leadership

Gratitude does not have to be grand gestures, it can be small, meaningful moments. A handwritten note, a verbal acknowledgment, or a moment of reflection on what has gone well can significantly impact both you and those around you. Leadership is not just about driving results; it is about valuing and recognizing the people who make those results possible.

Action Step: Write a gratitude letter to a mentor, team member, or someone who has positively influenced your leadership.

_____

_____

_____

_____

_____

_____

_____

_____

_____

_____

_____

_____

_____

_____

_____

_____

"Gratitude turns what we have into enough."

—Melody Beattie

Journal Entry: What are you most grateful for in your leadership journey?

_____

_____

_____

_____

_____

_____

_____

_____

_____

_____

_____

_____

_____

_____

_____

_____

Week 39: Leadership Longevity Strategies

__Mini Lesson:__ Sustaining leadership growth over time.

Some leaders reach a milestone and stop growing, believing they have arrived at their final destination. However, true leadership is a continuous process of learning, evolving, and adapting. The most impactful leaders never stop seeking knowledge, refining their skills, and challenging themselves.

To sustain leadership longevity, you must commit to ongoing professional and personal development. This may include attending conferences, reading leadership books, networking with peers, mentoring others, or engaging in reflective practices. Great leaders are lifelong learners.

Action Step: Identify and commit to one long-term leadership habit that will support your continued growth.

_____

_____

_____

_____

_____

_____

_____

_____

_____

_____

_____

_____

_____

_____

_____

_____

_____

"Leadership is a marathon, not a sprint."
—John C. Maxwell

Journal Entry: What long-term strategies can help sustain your leadership impact?

_____

_____

_____

_____

_____

_____

_____

_____

_____

_____

_____

_____

_____

_____

_____

_____

_____

Week 40: The Importance of Emotional Intelligence

Mini Lesson: Understanding and improving emotional intelligence in leadership.

Emotional intelligence (EI) is one of the most critical leadership skills. Leaders with high emotional intelligence communicate more effectively, build stronger relationships, and handle stress and conflict with grace.

Key components of emotional intelligence include:

- Self-awareness: Recognizing your emotions and their impact on leadership.
- Self-regulation: Managing emotional responses to foster productive outcomes.

- Empathy: Understanding and responding to the emotions of others.
- Social skills: Building relationships, resolving conflicts, and leading effectively.
- Motivation: Maintaining focus and drive for long-term goals.

Leaders who actively develop emotional intelligence create environments where trust, collaboration, and resilience thrive.

Action Step: During your next three conversations—whether personal or professional—intentionally practice active listening by giving your full attention, withholding judgment, and reflecting back what you hear. At the same time, tune into your emotional responses and the emotions of others, noting how emotional awareness influences the outcome of each interaction.

_____

_____

_____

_____

_____

_____

_____

_____

"Emotional intelligence is the key to both personal and professional success."

—Daniel Goleman

Journal Entry: How does emotional intelligence shape your leadership style?

_____

_____

_____

_____

_____

_____

_____

_____

_____

_____

_____

_____

_____

_____

_____

_____

_____

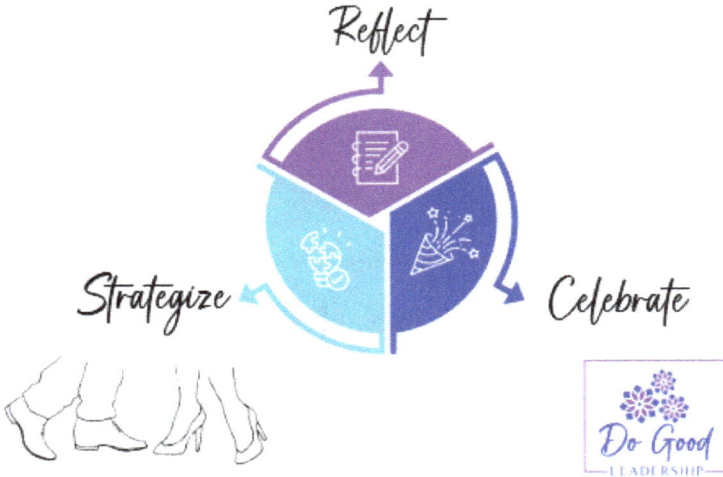

The Leadership Dance

Reflect

Strategize

Celebrate

Do Good
LEADERSHIP

Month 11 –
Reflect, Celebrate & Strategize

As leaders, we often focus on what's next without taking the time to recognize how far we've come. This month is about pausing to reflect, celebrating progress, and strategically planning for the future. Leadership is a journey filled with growth, challenges, and milestones, and recognizing those milestones is essential for motivation, confidence, and continued success. Taking the time to acknowledge achievements—both big and small—reinforces a culture of continuous improvement and allows you to appreciate the dedication and effort it took to get here. Gratitude plays a vital role in leadership, not only in acknowledging the contributions of others but also in recognizing the support, lessons, and opportunities that have shaped your path. By embracing gratitude, leaders cultivate a positive, people-centered leadership style that strengthens relationships and inspires those around them.

Reflection is not just about looking back; it's about using insights to shape the future. This month, you will evaluate your leadership approach to identify what's working, what needs refinement, and how to continue evolving as a leader. Leadership is never static; it requires adjustment, self-awareness, and adaptability. You will strategize for the future, developing a long-term leadership plan that aligns with your values, vision, and aspirations. This process will ensure that as you move forward, you do so with purpose, clarity, and a renewed sense of direction. Leadership is a continuous journey, and the best leaders are those who reflect, learn, and refine their approach while keeping their eyes on the future.

Week 41 focuses on recognizing leadership milestones, encouraging you to pause and celebrate the progress you've made on your leadership journey. You'll reflect on both big achievements and small wins, acknowledging the growth, resilience, and impact you've built along the way. Week 42 highlights the role of gratitude in leadership, teaching you how practicing gratitude—both toward others and yourself—strengthens relationships, fosters a positive team culture, and enhances your leadership fulfillment. You'll explore how gratitude, when practiced intentionally, becomes a powerful tool for authentic, people-centered leadership. Week 43 centers on evaluating and refining your leadership approach, reminding you that great leaders are always evolving. You'll reflect on your current leadership effectiveness, seek feedback, and identify one area where you can adapt and improve for greater long-term impact. Week 44 emphasizes planning for the future of leadership, guiding you to develop a strategy for continued growth. You'll assess where you are, where you want to go, and how to align your leadership vision with purpose-driven goals, setting the stage for a meaningful and sustainable leadership journey in the year ahead.

Week 41: Recognizing Leadership Milestones

> ***Mini Lesson:*** Celebrating achievements and recognizing growth.

One of the most overlooked aspects of leadership is pausing to recognize and celebrate progress. Too often, leaders focus on what still needs to be done, rather than acknowledging how far they have come. Recognizing leadership milestones is not about seeking external validation or grand celebrations; rather, it is about acknowledging your own journey, effort, and growth. These milestones can be as significant as earning a leadership position or as subtle as gaining confidence in speaking up during meetings. Leadership development is a continuous process, and every step forward—no matter how small—matters. Reflecting on your achievements fosters self-confidence, combats imposter syndrome, and provides motivation to keep moving forward.

Success is not only measured by titles or accolades but also by the lessons learned and the impact made along the way. Consider the personal and professional obstacles you have overcome, the challenges you have tackled, and the people you have positively influenced. Take time to reflect on the moments that shaped your leadership journey, whether it was successfully leading a team project, mentoring a colleague, or simply making a difficult but necessary decision. If you do not take ownership of your progress, no one else will. Celebrate your leadership evolution, recognize your resilience, and use your milestones as stepping stones toward even greater achievements.

Action Step: List your leadership milestones and celebrate them. Keep a running record of achievements, both big and small.

_____

_____

_____

_____

_____

_____

_____

_____

_____

_____

_____

_____

_____

_____

_____

_____

_____

_____

"Celebrate what you want to
see more of."
—Tom Peters

Journal Entry: What leadership milestones have you achieved this year?

_____

_____

_____

_____

_____

_____

_____

_____

_____

_____

_____

_____

_____

_____

_____

_____

_____

_____

Week 42: The Role of Gratitude in Leadership

> *Mini Lesson:* Practicing gratitude as a leadership tool.

Gratitude is one of the most powerful leadership tools that can transform not only your mindset but also your team's culture. It is more than just saying "thank you" or acknowledging people when expected—it is an intentional practice that strengthens relationships, builds trust, and fosters a positive work environment. When leaders show authentic gratitude, they create an atmosphere where team members feel valued, motivated, and empowered to contribute at their highest level. A simple act of recognition can inspire loyalty, encourage engagement, and enhance overall team morale.

However, gratitude in leadership is not just about others, it's also about self-reflection. Leaders must practice self-gratitude, acknowledging their own progress, resilience, and ability to navigate challenges. Recognizing what you have achieved, who has helped you along the way, and how your experiences have shaped you allows for a growth-oriented perspective. Integrating gratitude into daily leadership practices, whether through small gestures, written notes, or verbal recognition—creates a culture of appreciation and respect. When gratitude becomes a habit, leadership becomes more authentic, people-centered, and impactful.

Action Step: Express gratitude to those who have supported your leadership growth.

_____

_____

_____

_____

_____

_____

_____

_____

_____

_____

_____

_____

_____

_____

_____

_____

"Gratitude is not only the greatest of virtues but the parent of all others."
—Cicero

Journal Entry: How has gratitude influenced your leadership journey?

_____

_____

_____

_____

_____

_____

_____

_____

_____

_____

_____

_____

_____

_____

_____

_____

_____

Week 43: Evaluating and Refining Your Leadership Approach

> ***Mini Lesson:*** Reflecting on leadership effectiveness and areas of improvement.

Strong leaders are not those who believe they have all the answers, but those who continuously reflect, adapt, and refine their leadership approach. Effective leadership is an evolving journey, requiring self-awareness, adaptability, and a willingness to learn from both successes and failures. Too often, leaders fall into the trap of rigidity, believing that their initial approach should remain unchanged. However, the best leaders understand that growth comes from evaluating what is working and what needs improvement. This self-awareness leads to greater effectiveness, stronger relationships, and a more impactful leadership style.

Refining leadership does not mean imitating others; it means developing your unique, authentic leadership approach. Many leaders, especially women, feel pressured to conform to a traditional, often masculine style of leadership, but success lies in embracing your natural strengths, communication style, and values. Take time to assess how you lead, how you manage challenges, and how others respond to your leadership. Be open to constructive feedback, analyze your decision-making patterns, and seek opportunities to grow in areas that need improvement. Leadership is about continuous refinement, and those willing to adapt will have the greatest long-term impact.

Action Step: Seek feedback and implement one improvement.

_____

_____

_____

_____

_____

_____

_____

_____

_____

_____

_____

_____

_____

_____

_____

_____

_____

_____

"Examine what is said, not who speaks."
—African Proverb

Journal Entry: How can you refine your leadership for greater impact?

_____

_____

_____

_____

_____

_____

_____

_____

_____

_____

_____

_____

_____

_____

_____

_____

Week 44: Planning for the Future of Leadership

> ***Mini Lesson:*** Developing a strategy for long-term leadership growth.

Leadership is not about reaching a final destination—it is about continuous progress, adaptability, and long-term vision. A great leader does not simply respond to the present but proactively plans for the future. Many leaders spend their time solving immediate problems, but those who sustain success think ahead, anticipate challenges, and set clear, strategic goals. Planning for leadership growth means assessing where you are now, where you want to go, and what steps will get you there. This process requires introspection, foresight, and commitment to self-improvement.

As leadership evolves, so must your strategy. The goals you set today may shift as you gain new experiences, responsibilities, and insights. Flexibility is key—while long-term vision is essential, the path to achieving it may change. Identify areas where you want to grow, whether it is expanding your leadership influence, improving communication, or developing future leaders within your team. Create a leadership vision that aligns with your purpose and values and take intentional steps toward making that vision a reality. Leadership does not stop at achieving a title, it continues through purpose-driven action and meaningful impact.

Action Step: Set aside dedicated time this week to begin drafting a leadership vision plan for the next year. Start by identifying three key goals or initiatives you'd like to pursue—these can be ideas in progress or areas you feel called to grow in. Don't worry about having it fully developed; focus on capturing your aspirations, potential projects, and the impact you hope to make over the next 12 months.

_____

_____

_____

_____

_____

_____

_____

_____

_____

_____

_____

_____

_____

_____

"The best way to predict the future is to create it."

—Peter Drucker

Journal Entry: What leadership goals will you set for the upcoming year?

_____

_____

_____

_____

_____

_____

_____

_____

_____

_____

_____

_____

_____

_____

_____

_____

_____

Month 12 – Vision & Goal Setting for Impactful Leadership

As we enter the final month of this leadership journey, the focus shifts to vision and goal setting for long-term impact. Leadership is not just about what you have accomplished thus far, but about where you are going next. This month provides an opportunity to step back, reflect, and intentionally plan for the future. Too often, leaders get caught up in the day-to-day responsibilities and forget to strategically align their goals with their purpose. By creating a clear and compelling vision, leaders can set the foundation for sustainable growth, continued development, and lasting influence.

This month's lessons will guide you through establishing a long-term leadership vision, aligning daily actions with leadership purpose, and implementing strategies to sustain leadership growth year-round.

Week 45 focuses on creating a strategic vision for the future, guiding you to craft a vivid, personal leadership vision that serves as your north star. You'll reflect on the leader you want to become over the next five years and define the impact you want to create, aligning your daily choices with long-term aspirations. Week 46 highlights aligning goals with leadership purpose, showing you how to break down your big-picture vision into clear, actionable goals. You'll set three specific, measurable leadership goals for the coming year and connect them to daily habits that ensure steady progress toward meaningful outcomes. Week 47 centers on sustaining leadership growth year-round, reminding you that leadership is an ongoing journey, not a finish line. You'll identify one consistent habit to support your continuous growth, ensuring you stay adaptable, reflective, and committed to excellence over time. Week 48 emphasizes your leadership legacy and moving forward with purpose, inviting you to reflect on the lasting impact you want to leave. You'll define how you want to be remembered as a leader, assess whether your current actions align with that vision, and commit to leading with authenticity, influence, and heart.

Finally, you will define your leadership legacy, ensuring that the impact you have made continues beyond your immediate role. Your leadership journey does not end here; it evolves, expands, and shapes the future for those who follow in your footsteps. The key takeaway for this month is intentionality—what kind of leader do you want to be moving forward, and how will you take action to make it happen? Through this process, you will develop a roadmap for continued success and ensure that your leadership journey remains purposeful and impactful.

Do Good
LEADERSHIP

Week 45: Creating a Strategic Vision for the Future

> ***Mini Lesson:*** Understanding the importance of long-term vision in leadership.

Leadership is about more than the present moment, it is about crafting a vision for the future that keeps you motivated, aligned, and continuously growing. A sharp vision serves as a north star, guiding your decisions, actions, and leadership development over time. It is not just about setting goals; it is about envisioning the kind of leader you aspire to become and the impact you want to have. Without a vision, leadership can feel reactive, scattered, or aimless. But when you see yourself in that future position, your brain begins to work toward making it a reality, helping you align daily choices with long-term aspirations.

Your vision must be clear, compelling, and deeply personal. The more vividly you can see it, feel it, and define it, the more likely you are to take consistent actions toward achieving it. Think about the leader you want to be in five years. What do you want to be known for? What kind of teams will you build? What legacy will you create? Writing your personal leadership vision statement will help turn abstract ideas into a tangible roadmap for your journey ahead.

Action Step: Write a personal leadership vision statement for the next five years. Be as detailed and vivid as possible, describe the leader you will become and the impact you will have.

_____

_____

_____

_____

_____

_____

_____

_____

_____

_____

_____

_____

_____

"Where there is no vision,
the people perish."
—Proverbs 29:18

Journal Entry: What does success look like for you in five years?

_____

_____

_____

_____

_____

_____

_____

_____

_____

_____

_____

_____

_____

_____

_____

_____

_____

_____

_____

_____

Week 46: Aligning Goals with Leadership Purpose

> ***Mini Lesson:*** Connecting daily actions to long-term leadership goals.

A compelling vision provides direction, but goals provide structure. However, many leaders struggle because their goals remain too broad or vague, making it difficult to take meaningful action. The key to success is breaking down long-term aspirations into actionable, measurable steps. A goal without a plan is merely a wish. Leadership requires intentional daily actions that support your overarching purpose and ensure steady progress toward your vision.

To move forward effectively, consider setting three specific, measurable leadership goals for the upcoming year. But do not stop there—connect these goals to daily habits. If your goal is to improve team collaboration, what daily or weekly actions will reinforce it? If you want to expand your leadership influence, how will you build relationships, seek mentorship, or engage in professional development? Your leadership growth is the result of small, intentional choices repeated consistently.

Action Step: Set **three specific, measurable leadership goals** for the coming year. Then, identify the **daily actions** that will help you achieve them.

_____

_____

_____

_____

_____

_____

_____

_____

_____

_____

_____

_____

_____

_____

_____

_____

"Goals are the fuel in the furnace of achievement."
—Brian Tracy

Journal Entry: How do your leadership goals align with your overall purpose?

_____

_____

_____

_____

_____

_____

_____

_____

_____

_____

_____

_____

_____

_____

_____

_____

Week 47: Sustaining Leadership Growth Year-Round

Mini Lesson: Developing habits that ensure continued leadership growth.

Leadership is not a one-time achievement, it is a lifelong journey of growth, learning, and adaptability. Many leaders reach a milestone and stop developing, assuming they have "made it." However, true leadership requires constant evolution. To sustain growth year-round, leaders must actively cultivate habits that reinforce their development. This includes continuous learning, seeking new challenges, and remaining open to feedback.

One of the most effective ways to sustain leadership growth is to develop and commit to a habit that supports leadership excellence. This might involve reading leadership books regularly, attending professional development workshops, mentoring others, or setting aside time for reflection. The key is consistency. Small habits, repeated over time, create exponential impact.

Action Step: Identify one habit that will support your ongoing leadership growth and commit to practicing it consistently.

_____

_____

_____

_____

_____

_____

_____

_____

_____

_____

_____

_____

_____

_____

_____

_____

_____

_____

"Success is the sum of small efforts,
repeated day in and day out."
—Robert Collier

Journal Entry: What is one habit you've identified that will support your ongoing leadership growth? Why did you choose this habit, and how do you plan to practice it consistently in your daily routine? Reflect on how this habit could positively impact your leadership over time.

_____

_____

_____

_____

_____

_____

_____

_____

_____

_____

_____

_____

_____

_____

_____

Week 48: Your Leadership Legacy – Moving Forward with Purpose

> *Mini Lesson:* Defining the impact you want
> to leave as a leader.

Leadership is not about titles, awards, or personal accolades—it is about the impact you have on others. The greatest leaders are not remembered for their positions, but for the lives they touched, the teams they empowered, and the positive culture they created. Your leadership legacy is built in the everyday moments—in the way you support your colleagues, how you navigate challenges, and how you develop future leaders.

Defining your leadership legacy requires deep reflection. What do you want people to remember about your leadership? How do you want your contributions to be recognized? What values will define your leadership brand? The answers to these questions will help you align your actions with your impact. By crafting a leadership legacy statement, you create a powerful commitment to leading with authenticity, purpose, and long-term influence.

Action Step: Write a leadership legacy statement outlining how you want to be remembered as a leader. Reflect on whether your current actions align with the impact you desire to leave.

_____

_____

_____

_____

_____

_____

_____

_____

_____

_____

_____

_____

_____

_____

_____

_____

_____

_____

"Carve your name on hearts,
not tombstones."
—Shannon L. Alder

Journal Entry: What lasting impact do you want to have on those you lead?

_____

_____

_____

_____

_____

_____

_____

_____

_____

_____

_____

_____

_____

_____

_____

_____

Next Steps

SECTION FIVE: NEXT STEPS FOR THE NEWLY EMPOWERED LEADER

Embracing Leadership Beyond the First Year, Refining Strategies, and Expanding Impact

You have spent the past 48 weeks developing, strengthening, and elevating your leadership, but your journey is far from over. True leadership is an ongoing process of refinement, growth, and influence. This section is dedicated to helping you transition from learning to leading at an even greater scale, ensuring that your leadership impact extends beyond your immediate role.

Now that you have built a solid foundation, it is time to focus on expanding your influence, becoming a thought leader, fostering a sustainable leadership community, and defining your legacy. This phase is about stepping fully into your power and potential—leading with confidence, adaptability, and a commitment to continuous learning. Whether you are looking to mentor others, share your insights on a larger platform, or solidify your long-term leadership goals, these next steps will equip you with strategies to sustain and expand your leadership impact for years to come.

Week 49 focuses on expanding your leadership influence, guiding you to explore new ways to broaden your reach and amplify your impact beyond your immediate circle. You'll consider how to share your insights, mentor others, or advocate for positive change in your field, taking meaningful action to extend your leadership beyond your current role. Week 50 highlights becoming a thought leader in your field, encouraging you to identify your niche and establish yourself as a credible, influential voice. You'll reflect on how to share your expertise—whether through writing, speaking, or engaging in industry conversations—to inspire others and drive meaningful dialogue. Week 51 centers on building a sustainable leadership community, showing you how to intentionally nurture a network of mentors, peers, and emerging leaders. You'll explore how collaborative relationships fuel growth, elevate others, and create a thriving leadership ecosystem that supports long-term success. Week 52 emphasizes leading with legacy and purpose, inviting you to reflect on the lasting impact you want to leave behind. You'll define what leadership means to you, how you want to be remembered, and how your value-driven actions today can shape a better future for those who follow.

This is where you shift from leadership growth to leadership mastery—fully embracing your role as a confident, adaptable, and visionary leader who inspires positive change. Let's take these final steps together, ensuring that your leadership journey continues to evolve and thrive!

Week 49: Expanding Your Leadership Influence

> ***Mini Lesson:*** Identifying new ways to broaden your leadership reach.

Leadership is not confined to a title or position; it is a way of living, thinking, and engaging with those around you. True leadership influence extends beyond your immediate team and organization, reaching individuals, industries, and even communities. This week, the focus is on identifying how you can broaden your leadership reach and amplify your impact. Consider ways in which you can mentor emerging leaders, contribute your insights through writing or speaking, or advocate for positive change in your field. Expanding your leadership reach does not necessarily mean taking on more responsibilities, it means leveraging your experiences, knowledge, and strengths to create meaningful opportunities for others.

Think about where your leadership could have a greater impact. Is there a mentorship program you can join or create? Could you guest lecture at a university, present at a conference, or start your own professional network? Maybe you've been thinking about launching a podcast, writing a book, or developing an online course to share your expertise. Whatever avenue you choose, the goal is to take action and move beyond your immediate circle. Leadership is most effective when shared—whom can you inspire, support, and guide as you continue your own growth?

Action Step: Create a plan to share your leadership insights with a wider audience. Define who that audience is and the best way to reach them.

_____

_____

_____

_____

_____

_____

_____

_____

_____

_____

_____

_____

_____

_____

"Leadership is not about being in charge.
It is about taking care of
those in your charge."
—Simon Sinek

Journal Entry: How can you extend your leadership impact beyond your immediate sphere?

_____

_____

_____

_____

_____

_____

_____

_____

_____

_____

_____

_____

_____

_____

_____

_____

_____

Week 50: Becoming a Thought Leader in Your Field

Mini Lesson: Establishing credibility and influence as a leader in your industry.

Being a great leader is about more than just managing people—it is about shaping ideas, influencing conversations, and driving change in your field. Becoming a thought leader means honing in on a specific area of expertise, developing deep knowledge in that space, and sharing valuable insights with others. Many leaders make the mistake of trying to be knowledgeable about everything, but true thought leadership comes from focusing on one area where you can offer unique insights and solutions.

Start by identifying your niche. What are you passionate about? What topics do colleagues, students, or team members frequently ask for your advice on? Your niche could be educational leadership, conflict resolution, innovative teaching practices, or empowering women in leadership. Once you have defined your space, take the next step—write, speak, and engage in conversations that position you as an expert. This could be through blog posts, social media, conference presentations, guest appearances on podcasts, or writing for professional publications. Being a thought leader is not about knowing everything—it is about consistently sharing valuable insights and inspiring others to think differently.

Action Step: Write or speak publicly about a key leadership lesson. This could be at a conference, on a podcast, in an article, or through social media.

"It is worth remembering that it is often the small steps, not the giant leaps, that bring about the most lasting change."
—Queen Elizabeth II

Journal Entry: What steps can you take to position yourself as a thought leader?

_____

_____

_____

_____

_____

_____

_____

_____

_____

_____

_____

_____

_____

_____

_____

_____

_____

Week 51: Building a Sustainable Leadership Community

Mini Lesson: Creating and nurturing a leadership network.

Great leaders don't work in isolation—they surround themselves with other strong, insightful, and inspiring leaders. A sustainable leadership community is built through consistent connection, collaboration, and mutual support. It is not just about networking; it is about forming relationships that are meaningful and enduring. This week's focus is on how you can intentionally build and maintain a network of leaders who challenge and support you.

Your leadership network does not have to be formal—it can be a combination of mentors, peers, and emerging leaders that you check in with regularly. Are you maintaining connections with colleagues from conferences? Are you following up with past mentors and mentees? Have you built relationships beyond your own organization or industry? Take time to assess your leadership network and identify ways to strengthen and sustain it. A thriving leadership community allows for collaborative learning, shared problem-solving, and the ability to elevate others. Who are three people you can support in their leadership journey?

Action Step: Identify three people to mentor or support in their leadership journey. These could be mentees, peers, or new connections.

_____

_____

_____

_____

_____

_____

_____

_____

_____

_____

_____

_____

_____

_____

_____

_____

"A leader is best when people barely know he exists, when his work is done, his aim fulfilled, they will say: we did it ourselves."
—Lao Tzu

Journal Entry: How can you foster a leadership community that thrives beyond your involvement?

_____

_____

_____

_____

_____

_____

_____

_____

_____

_____

_____

_____

_____

_____

_____

_____

Week 52: Leading with Legacy and Purpose

> ***Mini Lesson:*** Leaving a legacy through
> purposeful leadership.

Your leadership journey is not just about the actions you take today—it is about the impact you leave behind. True leadership is about serving others, empowering those around you, and creating a lasting, positive change in your organization, community, and industry. As you reach this final stage, reflect on the legacy you want to leave. What do you want people to say about your leadership? How will your efforts today shape the future for those who follow in your footsteps?

A leadership legacy is built through consistent, value-driven actions. It is about mentoring others, fostering a culture of integrity and inclusivity, and making decisions that align with your greater purpose. It is not about the awards you receive or the titles you hold; it is about the lives you impact. This week, take time to define what leadership means to you and how you want to be remembered.

Action Step: Write a letter to your future self about your leadership journey. Reflect on your growth, challenges, and the impact you want to leave behind.

_____

_____

_____

_____

_____

_____

_____

_____

_____

_____

_____

_____

_____

_____

_____

_____

_____

"Legacy is not what I did for myself. It's what I'm doing for the next generation."
—Vitor Belfort

Journal Entry: What is the legacy you hope to leave as a leader?

_____

_____

_____

_____

_____

_____

_____

_____

_____

_____

_____

_____

_____

_____

_____

_____

The Leadership Dance

Congratulations!

Reflect

Strengthen

Elevate

Do Good LEADERSHIP

Step Out

Step In

Step Up

Step Back

Step Across

Step Away

Step Aside

Step Together

Step Forward

Congratulations! You Have Completed Your 52-Week Leadership Journey

Whether you took it one week at a time or doubled up on some of the lessons, you have reached the last stage of this transformative journey. Over the past 52 weeks, you have reflected, strengthened your foundation, elevated your leadership, and renewed your purpose for long-term impact. Through structured activities, personal journaling, and intentional self-reflection, you have deepened your understanding of what it truly means to be an empowered and authentic leader.

What Comes Next?

Your leadership development does not stop here, it is an ongoing process of learning, growth, and refinement. As you move forward, consider these next steps:

- Continue the Practice – Leadership is not a destination but a continuous evolution. Keep reflecting, learning, and developing your skills.
- Share Your Knowledge – Great leaders develop other leaders. Mentor, guide, and support those who are just beginning their leadership journey.
- Stay Accountable – Revisit your goals regularly, assess your growth, and use your leadership vision as a compass for future success.
- Lead with Purpose – Leadership is not about titles or positions—it is about making an impact. Stay true to your values and lead with authenticity.

Your Leadership Legacy

The mark you leave as a leader is shaped by your daily actions, decisions, and mindset. True leadership is about empowering, serving, and transforming—not only yourself but also those around you. As you continue forward, remember to step up, step in, step out, and lead with confidence, courage, and clarity. This journey has prepared you to embrace challenges, inspire others, and drive meaningful change.

Join the Do Good Leadership Movement-
Visit www.drstephanieduguid.com

Your leadership journey is just beginning! If you're ready to expand your impact, continue your growth, and connect with other like-minded professionals, we invite you to join the Do Good Leadership community. Here's how you can get involved:

- Engage with Like-Minded Leaders – Connect with professionals who share your passion for leadership and personal growth.
- Participate in Exclusive Leadership Workshops – Gain access to innovative training, mentorship, and development opportunities.
- Receive Ongoing Support & Insights – Stay informed with leadership strategies, tools, and best practices to help you lead with confidence.
- Make a Difference – Use your leadership to empower others and create a lasting impact in your organization and community.

Invite Dr. Stephanie Duguid to Speak at Your Next Event

Dr. Stephanie Duguid is an inspiring speaker, leadership expert, and advocate for exponentially elevating leadership impact. She brings practical insights, real-world experience, and motivational energy to every audience, helping individuals and organizations unlock their full potential.

If you're looking for a keynote speaker, workshop facilitator, or leadership coach, Dr. Duguid is available to speak at conferences, corporate events, leadership summits, and educational institutions. Her sessions are designed to engage, inspire, and equip leaders with actionable strategies to transform their leadership journey.

Take the Next Step

Visit Do Good Leadership at www.drstephanieduguid.com to join our community and continue your journey of exponential leadership growth. Contact us today to book Dr. Stephanie Duguid for your next event and take your team's leadership to the next level! We cannot wait to see how you step forward, lead with purpose, and elevate your leadership impact!

Meet Dr. Stephanie Duguid

Dr. Stephanie Duguid, an expert in Educational Leadership, International Best-Selling Author, and a recognized leader among professional women, is the owner/founder of Do Good Leadership.

With over 100 conference invitations and numerous appearances at colleges and universities nationwide, Dr. Stephanie is a renowned speaker, known for her expertise in positive educational leadership and effective communication. Her sessions promise dynamic interactions, research-based content, thought-provoking engagement, and actionable takeaways. Dr. Stephanie's unique abilities as a strategist and connector empower clients to create truly exceptional outcomes.

Drawing from decades of experience in K-12 and Higher Education, Dr. Stephanie's communication skills, along with her roles as a national speaker, author, and consultant, make her a sought-after authority on leadership. Her insights have been featured in notable outlets, including "America Tonight with Kate Delaney," and highlighted in Pearson Higher Education, McGraw-Hill Higher Ed, and others. As the creator and host of the "Empowering Women in Educational Leadership" radio show, podcast, and blog, she engages high-profile guests, including college and university presidents, educational technology leaders, and national executive directors in education. Her most popular themes have been Overcoming Imposter Syndrome, The Role of Mentorship, and Cultivating a Culture of Empowerment.

In her highly acclaimed keynote, "Exponentially Elevate Your Impact as an Educational Leader," Dr. Stephanie talks about defining your Purpose and Vision as a woman in educational leadership. Audiences are captivated by the value she brings, her relatability, and her deep understanding of their individual experiences as an educator. In her keynote, she addresses the topics of Positive Leadership, Mindset, Optimism, and Managing Conflicts with Grace.

Furthermore, Dr. Stephanie is a consistent advisor to educational leadership programs, leveraging her background as a former chief academic officer and state educational leader. Her educational contributions have earned her accolades, including the Excellence Award from the National Institute of Staff and Organizational Development.

Possessing a doctoral degree in educational leadership and a master's in curriculum and instruction, Dr. Stephanie has forged collaborations with esteemed institutions like Michigan State University and the University of West Alabama, creating pathways for students pursuing baccalaureate, master's, and doctoral degree programs.

Beyond her professional endeavors, Dr. Stephanie actively participates in leadership roles within educational organizations, including Delta Kappa Gamma. Her commitment to supporting students in education, nursing, and social work is evident through her local community college scholarship in memory of her mother.

www.ingramcontent.com/pod-product-compliance
Lightning Source LLC
Chambersburg PA
CBHW071330210326
41597CB00015B/1401